To Robin —
I hope you e...
It's my favorite...

SPEAKING OF
faith

INSIGHT PUBLISHING
SEVIERVILLE, TENNESSEE

SPEAKING OF

faith

Published by Insight Publishing Company
P.O. Box 4189
Sevierville, Tennessee 37864

10 9 8 7 6 5 4 3 2

Printed in The United States of America

ISBN: 1-60013-026-7

Table Of Contents

A Message From The Publisher

I have been involved in church ministry as a musician ever since I was a teenager. I've also been a church staff member for many years. I know how important it is to have faith and how essential it is to experiencing a fulfilled life.

My experience in the corporate world has taught me that many people are looking for answers to life's most important questions: Why am I here? Is there a purpose for my life? How do I make a difference in my world?

We have put together *Speaking of Faith* to help you answer these questions by taking a look at how others have answered them and how they've applied those answers in their own lives.

We searched for and found some of the most outstanding leaders from various walks of faith to be contributors to this book. During the conversations I had with these folks I decided to be bold and ask questions that would reveal in-depth, insightful, and truly inspiring answers. We believe their answers will help you make meaningful decisions about developing your own faith.

We hope you will find this book fascinating and helpful. It was put together with you in mind. Enjoy!

Interviews conducted by:
David E. Wright
President, International Speakers Network

Chapter One

JOANI TABOR

David Wright (Wright)

Today we're talking with Joani Tabor. Looking into a sea of faces Joani Tabor sings for the Lord, forever embracing her motto, "Nothing's Going To Steal My Joy." The impact on her listeners is unmistakable. With a bubbly personality, Joani conveys her enthusiastic faith in concert—a powerful presentation every time. Joani holds a Master's in Theology degree. Having taught voice, she speaks at colleges, universities, retreats, conventions, and seminars. Throughout her ministry Joani has had the opportunity to entertain presidents and national leaders. Joani combines sincerity with excellence of presentation. Her delightful multi-style mix of music renews the hearts of listeners regardless of their age. Joani's clear voice, which covers an astonishing four octaves, has been described as "intense vocal artistry."

Joani, welcome to *Speaking of Faith*.

Tabor

Thank you very much David.

Wright

Joani, tell us about your background.

Tabor

I grew up in Bramwell, a small town in the hills of southern West Virginia. My father, Phillip, inspired my love of music. I recall every night going to bed with music playing. My dad taught me to appreciate the artistry of all styles of music. Little did I know that God was preparing me for my future ministry.

My three siblings and I were in the band and chorus at Bramwell High School. I continue to play flute, keyboard, piano, and organ. My father died suddenly of cardiac arrest at thirty-two years of age. What a heritage and legacy my father left behind. His love of music passed on to me. Sometimes, especially early in my ministry, I could almost feel my daddy smiling down and saying, "I am so proud of you, Joani, way to go!"

My husband, Glenn, has been my greatest support system. I cannot and would not be in this ministry without his constant, unwavering encouragement. He has literally shared me with the entire world. I truly do not know many husbands who would do that.

Wright

Your ministry has taken you all over the world. What are some of your most memorable experiences?

Tabor

A year after my father's death, I came to Christ, and Jesus became my "Daddy." Every day after school, I would sit on my front porch swing and talk to Him about my day. I remember saying over and over, "Please don't let me live in this place, or marry anyone from here. I want to get out and do great things for you."

The Lord spoke to my heart one day and told me I would travel the world and sing to thousands of people. I said, "I just want to go to Hawaii." Little did I know that God's plans were so much bigger. God was stretching my faith. The more I have exercised a little faith, the more God has increased it over and over again.

When God called me to this ministry in 1990, I asked Him to let me sing in all fifty states. It took me six and a half years to accomplish that plan, so I made my plan bigger. I asked the Lord to let me sing and speak on every continent. That took another seven years.

To this date, I have ministered in all fifty states and in over thirty nations. My music has been played on over 900 stations in the United States. Seven point two million listeners in ninety-five countries hear my music on Quality Europe Radio FM. Short Wave Radio Network has made my music and ministry available to every nation on earth. I have appeared at the White House, the Crystal Cathedral, at Dollywood in Pigeon Forge, Tennessee, in Branson, Missouri, and at New Heritage USA. I have made over 3000 university, college, church, concert, convention, retreat, and seminar appearances. I have appeared on INSP (The Inspirational Network), The ACTS Network, Sky Angel Network, The Family Network, and have made over 100 television appearances. That is a long way from a porch swing in Bramwell, West Virginia!

Wright

I understand you're no stranger to tragedy, having lost your father at age eleven. What effect has that had on your life?

Tabor

The death of my father had both positive and negative effects on my life. At age eleven, I was trying to figure out who I was, why I was here—all of those questions every young person has when trying to reach maturity. For a long time I grieved about my father's death. He was my best friend and I loved him very much. It was difficult for me to accept that he was gone, never to return.

I often blamed myself. I felt that if I had just been a better girl he wouldn't have left me. Today I know this is a common thought process. Even now, it is difficult for me to remember his facial features or hear his laugh. I suppose I buried the pain so deeply that even good things have escaped my memory bank. It's hard to know who you are when half of you is gone.

On the other hand, his death made me stronger in a myriad of ways. He prepared me to understand God in a profound way. I felt that Dad understood me and we had a great connection. I could climb up on my daddy's knee and when I was bad, he loved me with a sad heart. When I was good, he loved me with a glad heart. But he always loved me. What a great visual of God and His grace. Dad's death prepared me for this journey of ministry the Lord had in mind that I knew nothing about. His death helped me to empathize with others who have suffered a loss. I learned that we must love people but depend on God. People weave in and out of our lives but He is constant.

Wright

In addition to the pain of losing your father at such an early age I understand that you've also lost a child and that your sister was killed in a car crash the day before her wedding. What impact did these events have on your faith?

Tabor

Losing my baby was an extraordinarily shocking event, of course, and one that shook me to my very core. In spite of the fact that I had been saved since I was twelve years old and had been married to a pastor for eight years, my faith was completely and utterly devastated. For the first time in my life I questioned whether there really was a God. I thought that if there was a God, why would He let such a horrible thing happen to me?

Of course, my first question to God was, "Why me?"

His response was one I did not like very much. He said, "Why *not* you, Joani?"

I had to understand, once and for all that God is sovereign. This means God does what He wants, when He wants, where He wants, and I don't tell Him what to do.

The loss of my baby plunged me into a deep, dark depression. Isolation, anger, doubt, anxiety, and fear filled my days and my nights. I was totally and completely overwhelmed. Because I was a pastor's wife, I went to church but I didn't get anything out of it. I went into the "habit mode" of Christianity.

The only reason I got up in the morning was because I had a three-year-old son who needed a mommy. All the while, Satan—the master of every bad idea I've ever had—was saying to me, "Take your three-year-old son and leave town and don't tell anybody where you're going." Even though I loved my husband, I knew he couldn't be married to a woman who doubted there was a God.

I made my preparations. I was going to leave on a Monday. On Friday I decided to do all the laundry in the house. I packed suitcases for my son and me and hid them under the bed so that when my husband returned from the church, hospital, or wherever he was that day, he would not see the evidence of my plan.

I folded the last load of laundry. As I crossed the threshold of my bedroom door, in my mind's eye I saw the rocking chair in the corner where I was going to rock my little girl. It became bigger than life; it was all I could see. I dropped the laundry on the floor and fell across my bed. I cried out to God and wailed for quite some time. Finally I looked up toward the ceiling as if it were toward heaven and said a simple prayer to God: "God, if you're really up there, and if you're really who you say you are, you're going to have to come and help me or I'm never going to serve you again."

God prompted me to get up off the bed, dry my tears, walk over to the dresser, and pick up His Word—the Bible. I sat in the rocker and even with a master's degree in theology and as a pastor's wife, I had no idea where to look. I let the Word fall open in my left hand. It fell open to a passage in the book of Psalms.

After reading the very first words of that passage, Jesus, the Great Physician, came and healed my broken heart. He gave me a glimpse into the future—someday I'm going to sit with my little girl in heaven by the River of Life. We're going to dangle our toes in the cool, clear stream. She's going to look at me and say, "Mommy, you won't believe what a great Daddy Jesus has been!"

I now know that my little girl is not in my past, she is in my future. We will be eternally together marching around the throne and praising God. So I'm encouraged by that. Who can grieve when your child is "partying with Jesus"?

I learned that no matter what I see with my eyes or hear with my ears, God is who He says He is and He can be trusted. Knowing that comforted me several years later after the death of Toni, my youngest sister. On her way to pick up my other sister, Rhoda, at the airport the day before her wedding, she was killed instantly in a car crash. I was flying in to sing at the wedding and had not yet arrived. During that tragic time, I simply looked back to the death of my baby and did not have to ask the same questions. Speaking of faith, I already knew who God was and that God can do what He wants to, when He wants to, and how He wants to. Even though I grieved her death, I was able to understand that God knows—truly knows—what is best for all of our lives.

Wright

You have been known to say it took a great leap of faith to get started on your current career path. Will you tell our readers how you got started and what part faith played in your decision?

Tabor

It's very interesting, David, because I am often asked that question of how I got started in my music ministry. The great leap of faith it took for me was unmistakable. I was content being a wife and raising my two children. I wasn't looking for an assignment from God. In fact, I was in a comfortable place. I was teaching vocal skills and was the pastor's wife. When He called me to this ministry, I resisted. I was distressed that God was going to shake up my world. I did not want to go to strange places, sleep on strange beds with strange pillows, and meet strange people. That was not what I thought my life should be.

In retrospect, my greatest fear was failure. I believe that most people in the church are afraid to fail! Consequently, when God comes to us with an assignment, we want to make every excuse in the book as to why we can't do it. We talk about our frailties, we talk about our lack of gifts, and we talk about our inabilities. However, I found out firsthand, if He calls us to something, He will give us the tools to accomplish it. This leap of faith taught me that we serve a successful God—one who has never failed. The late James Blackwood encouraged me to pursue this ministry after hearing me sing in Memphis, Tennessee. Mr. Blackwood remains a friend though he has gone home to be with the Lord.

Wright

You gained national recognition with an impressive Female Vocalist of the Year award. Your first professional recording contract featured a national release of, "Nothing's Going To Steal My Joy." I understand the song charted nationally, which is an amazing accomplishment for a new release from a new artist. Why do you feel this song has made such an impact on people?

Tabor

God often works in the simple things. The song, "Nothing's Going To Steal My Joy," impacts people because it contains a very simple message—a message of joy and hope.

Joy is very misunderstood. People mistakenly believe that joy depends on their circumstances. I'm glad that's not true. Joy is a free gift of God—a fruit of His Spirit. Just when we think we have it made, Satan comes in to steal, kill, and destroy. Daily we need to be reminded that, "the joy of the Lord is your strength" (Nehemiah 8:10). This simple song has touched more lives than any song I've ever recorded. Sometimes the simplest messages are the hardest to grasp. God is always speaking to us. I thank God He speaks to hearts through this song. After all, that's the only explanation for any success in songs or Christian ministry.

One of my greatest desires is for people to enjoy Jesus and revel in their faith journey. I always say you don't get "holy" in a hurry!

Wright

You have performed and then received accolades from many well-known people. Reverend Billy Graham has said that you were blessed with a remarkable musical gift and former First Lady, Nancy Reagan, says you are a very talented lady. So what factors do you feel have contributed to your success?

Tabor

My success is all about God, God, God!

His calling in my life has been, and continues to be, clear to me. I simply put my hand in His hand every single day because in His hand is success. If I walk with Him and follow Him—sometimes stumbling, sometimes tired, sometimes weary from the journey—and I never let go, God will always make me successful.

I know I have to be consistent, I have to have perseverance, and I have to love what I do. I've never lost that zeal and love for what I do. The calling of God is as fresh for me today as it was sixteen years ago when God called me to this ministry.

Wright

I understand that you have a passion for speaking at women's conferences and retreats. You focus much of your attention on these areas. Why do you feel speaking to women gives you such great satisfaction?

Tabor

I delight in seeing God transform lives and homes and marriages. I delight in seeing God take women who are weak and make them mighty women of valor. I delight in seeing Christian women who want to do great things for God.

One of my "pet peeves" in the church concerns the fact that we're told to do better, to read the Word more, to pray more, to be givers and servers, but we're never given the tools. I believe that if we're given proper tools, a child of God with a mind that is made up is powerful! God delights in that!

Wright

You hold a master's degree in theology, which is quite an accomplishment. What led you to choose this profession—this particular field?

Tabor

My interest has always been in the Word. I'm still a woman of the Word. My master's degree in theology doesn't make me any smarter than anyone else. I don't think God is at all impressed with our degrees, our gifts, or our abilities. I know that what impresses God is our character. Therefore, we should spend much more time on building character, realizing the Word builds godly character. I had made plans to become an English teacher and wanted to be in journalism. Surprise, surprise, God had other plans for me. I didn't choose theology—it chose me!

Wright

You're known for celebrating life through music as you spread your message of hope and encouragement. With all the tragedies in your life, how do you manage to hold on to your hope?

Tabor

I *choose* to—I choose to be happy. I choose to get out of my "pity parties." I get up every day and choose the abundant life. The world can give me a good life but only God gives me the *best* life. Do bad things only happen to bad people? That's the question I had to answer for myself. Bad things happen to good people—to *all* people. We're in trouble, or we've just gotten out of trouble, or we're getting ready to get into trouble—that's life. Always remember: there is no testimony without a test.

Wright

It's apparent that faith has played a big part in your life. You share your stories of things God has done for you over and over again. What can you tell our readers to inspire them to keep their faith?

Tabor

One of the topics I teach in my seminars is stress management. We live in a stressful world and there is no getting around that. Details, time crunches, traffic, children, marriages—all of these have their pressures. Christian psychologists have concluded that only about 8 percent of what stresses us will ever come to pass. Unfortunately, most Christians' "theme song" is "Why Pray When You Can Worry?" I recorded a song with this title several years ago. When listening to this song people realize that they are either a worrywart or are married to one.

We must stop looking at our difficulties because these problems become our gods. We must start looking at the God who can free us from our problems. Our constant dilemma is we limit Him by our lack of faith—our lack of trust.

I am convinced we have to learn to enjoy Jesus more. We have to enjoy the ride with Him and understand that it's an eternal ride. If we can look at life from God's point of view, truly we will have gained a little wisdom and a lot more joy.

Wright

You know, it's highly likely that someone reading this book is going through some of the same things that you went through—death, separation, divorce—many of the things that people have to struggle with to get through life. What advice would you give to our readers who are trying to get through something that is so difficult?

Tabor

Whether it is separation by death, divorce, or a separation because we've turned someone away, God gives us a natural grief process. We must fully experience the grief and learn the valuable lessons God is teaching. If we simply learn the lessons of faith, we will soon find ourselves in a different place with God and our Christianity.

I encourage people to read the Word, to get alone with God, to sit at His feet, bask in His presence, and wait upon the Lord. I am living proof that God will take something from nothing. I grew up in a very, very small place—in the hills of West Virginia. God is taking me to bigger and better and more wonderful things than I could have ever imagined. However, along the way I've experienced some of the same the pitfalls—hurt, anger, fear, and doubt—that all our readers have had or will have. I'll never live long enough here to completely stay out of trouble on this earth!

Wright

You have mentioned your father as a significant influence in your life. Besides your father, who has been the greatest influence in your life?

Tabor

No one ever has great success in life apart from others. That's very true in my life and ministry.

My grandmother, Edith Albert, was a great woman of faith. Even though her body was riddled with rheumatoid arthritis and diabetes, her faith in God never wavered. She taught me that God can do anything anytime He chooses. I now know she was teaching me about the sovereignty of God. It is dangerous territory when churches and individuals believe that God can do only what they tell Him.

I would go every day after school and brush my grandmother's hair; her health left her unable to do so. It's amazing how close you get to someone when you serve him or her every day. I touched her, but she touched me more. She went home to be with the Lord when I was only twelve years old. Her influence in my life is still palpable today.

Often Sunday school teachers and other leaders do not realize the influence they have on young minds. They are under-appreciated and are not often aware of the results of their hard work and diligent study. I'll never forget my junior Sunday school teacher, Vivian Peters. She had just finished Bible College and her excitement and knowledge of the Lord was truly contagious. Vivian made even learning about the kings in the Old Testament interesting; and everyone knows that's a miracle! She taught me to love and respect the Word of God and she made it come alive. A spark was ignited within me to do something great for God. At the age of only ten, I realized I served a big God.

When my father died, my mother, Shirley, was forced to raise four young children. As an adult, I am still realizing the influence my mother had on me during my early years. She is a strong woman who taught her children a very simple concept: If you place God first in everything, He'll supply all your needs. Mom lived this concept, not only in word but also in deed. I never saw my mother buy a new dress—she gave her tithes to God every week. She was faithful to the Lord's church and insisted that we be faithful also. I saw my mother give what little she had to others who were in greater need. She was never a whiner or complainer. She always stepped up to the plate to do whatever was necessary for the survival of her children.

Two of the people who had the most influence in my life are my children. Glenn III, my first-born, taught me how to take responsibility for someone other than myself. When I lost my baby, he was the only reason I got up in the morning. He needed a mom and I was it.

Our son was born on New Year's Day. People often ask me, "Don't you wish he was born the day before so you could get the tax deduction?"

I always reply, "I'm married to a pastor and we didn't need it!"

Glenn is such a fun, creative, wonderful young man. He has a positive outlook on life and is an extremely hard worker. He engineers and produces all my musical projects. He has learned to work with me "up close and personal." Our son and his wife, Susan, have given us two precious delights—Madelenn Marie and Julia Grace.

Our daughter, Joalenn, continues to amaze me. She was God's gift to me after the loss of my child. She was a continuation of my healing from that devastation. Even though she is totally independent, she continues to value the wisdom of her mom and dad. I'm intrigued by her attention to detail and her loyalty to family and friends. Joalenn is a special education teacher at the same middle school she attended. They still like her! Her constant companion is her beautiful Silky Terrier, Moneke.

Obviously, the most influential person in my life is my husband, Glenn. This ministry would not be possible without him. He is my constant prayer partner and faithful confidant. Glenn has taught me more about the Bible and the truths of God's Word than anyone. He is a great speaker and teacher in his own right. Coming from a childhood where everyone I trusted had left me, Glenn taught me to trust again. He also taught me to believe in myself and to know that I am capable of doing more than I dreamed possible. Glenn is a very stable, loyal, and dependable person. He was born forty and he will die forty!

"No man is an island" and neither is any woman. These people and many others have molded and shaped who I am. I have thousands of prayer partners who pray for me every week. Just as these people have encouraged and influenced me, my prayer is to do the same for others. I'm convinced that we will never know all those we have influenced until we touch the face of God.

Wright
Your ministry is more varied than just presenting musical concerts. What exactly is Joani Tabor Ministries?

Tabor
It is true that I do musical concerts in churches, convention centers, conference centers, and other venues. "Joani Tabor Ministries" is about training women. I speak and lecture at women's retreats, con-

ferences, banquets, and on college campuses. I want to teach women that their role in the church is important and crucial to the success of the Kingdom. Using the Word of God and relevant topics, I try to enhance their capabilities as wives, mothers, and businesswomen. Traveling the country and the world, I try to encourage pastors and their wives, ministry leaders, and missionaries.

Another aspect of my ministry is choir and praise team retreats. With my background in teaching vocals skills, I am able to give practical advice in presentation and communication. My major thrust is to get them to understand that their only job is to take people to the throne room of glory and deposit them there. In group ministry, there are no "big I's" and "little you's"—everyone has important contributions to make. We must be focused on *Him* and not on performance only.

From my perspective, marriage is definitely a neglected area in our churches. To address this neglect, I have written seminars for marriage retreats. Men must learn what women need and women must take the time to learn what men need. Until we understand what our spouses need, we can never meet those needs. Or better yet, we must acknowledge that God can meet those needs through us. After all, God has called us to serve one another.

Many have commented about my ability to motivate. Community businesses and organizations provide an opportunity for me to speak on stress relief, teamwork, time management, and successful strategies for living.

One of my biggest passions is meeting the needs of others, therefore, every Christmas we supply "love packs" for an orphanage in India. Joani Tabor Ministries helps in natural disasters. We provide musical and teaching materials for prisons. Every year we take a mission trip and try to touch those outside our own country. Besides speaking and singing, we assist missionaries in evangelistic efforts in the countries where they serve.

It is a privilege and honor to serve God worldwide. He opens the doors and I try to be faithful to walk through them.

Wright

What an interesting conversation, what an interesting lady you are.

Tabor

Oh, thank you.

Wright

I've learned a lot here today—a lot of things I'm going to think about.

Tabor

I've shared from my heart. I hope it has been helpful and that it will encourage those who read this chapter.

Wright

Well, I appreciate the time you've spent with me today.

Tabor

I'm glad to be working with you, David, and I hope this will bless people's lives. That's the purpose of everything I do.

Wright

Today we have been talking with Joani Tabor and what a conversationalist she is. And what an inspiration to others she has become. She combines sincerity with excellence in her presentations. Her clear voice, which includes an astonishing four octaves, has been described as "intense vocal artistry." What a nice compliment.

Tabor

Thank you, David. I hope everyone will enjoy Jesus today and remember, "Nothing's Going to Steal My Joy!"

About the Author

Looking into a sea of faces, Joani Tabor sings for the Lord, forever embracing her motto, "Nothing's Gonna Steal My Joy." The impact on her listeners is unmistakable. Joani, with bubbling personality, conveys her enthusiastic faith in concert—and it is powerful. Worship music has the power to turn people to the heart of God and draw them to Him. Joani Tabor is a blessed individual who shares her voice with the world and the world responds. She has witnessed over 25,000 decisions for Christ in the past thirteen years and has no intention of stopping there.

Joani quickly gained national recognition with an impressive "Female Vocalist of the Year" and Gold Cross award-winning musical career. Her first professional recording contract featured a national release "Nothing's Gonna Steal My Joy." The song charted nationally, an amazing accomplishment for a release from a new artist. It was the first of many songs to chart on the national Christian music charts. She has completed numerous recording projects, a live video, and recordings of her seminar teachings. Her music has received stellar reviews from national Christian music magazines. Joani continues to merit accolades.

Joani holds a Master of Theology degree. Besides having taught voice, she speaks for colleges, universities, retreats, conventions, and seminars. Joani has a passion for women's conferences and retreats and focuses much of her attention in those areas. She has seen as many as three hundred respond to Christ in a single invitation.

Joani celebrates life through her music, spreading her message of hope and encouragement. Sharing Christ with others is what Joani Tabor is all about.

Joani Tabor
Phone: 540.562.5433
Phone: 704.525.5552
Email: joani@joanitabor.org
www.joanitabor.org

Chapter 2

DR. ROBERT SCHULLER

David E. Wright (Wright)

Robert Harold Schuller was born in Alton, Iowa. He was raised on his parent's farm nearby, in a small, close-knit community of Dutch Americans. Robert knew from the early age of four that he wanted to be a minister of the church.

After graduating from a tiny high school in nearby Newkirk, Iowa, he entered Hope College in Holland, Michigan, where he earned a Bachelor of Arts degree. Robert pursued his religious studies at Western Theological Seminary and in 1950 he received his Master of Divinity. The young Reverend Schuller married Arvella DeHann of Newkirk, and the newlyweds moved to Chicago where the newly ordained minister took up his first assignment as pastor of the Ivanhoe Reformed Church. During his ministry there the congregation grew from thirty-eight to over four hundred.

In 1955, Schuller's denomination, the Reformed Church of America (RCA), called on him to build a new congregation in Garden Grove, California. With only $500 in assets, he decided to rent a drive-in movie theater, the Orange Drive-in. On the first Sunday, one hundred persons attended services seated in their cars, while Reverend Schuller preached from the tarpaper roof of the snack bar. The Garden Grove congregation continued to grow.

When a larger building was needed, Rev. Schuller commissioned the renowned architect Phillip Johnson to build a new building, all of glass—the "Crystal Cathedral." After almost insurmountable difficulties, this 2,736-seat architectural marvel was dedicated in 1980, "To the Glory of Man for the Greater Glory of God." Today, one million people visit the Cathedral annually. Dr. Schuller is the author of over thirty books, six of which have found a place on the *New York Times* and *Publisher's Weekly* bestseller lists.

Dr. Schuller, welcome to *Speaking of Faith*.

Dr. Robert Schuller (Schuller)
Thank you, David.

Wright
Dr. Schuller, you have stated, "I learned from my dad to dream, even when the dream seems impossible." Would you tell us about your parents and what impact they had on your early life?

Schuller
Yes, my father and mother were, by all standards I guess, poor. They owned a farm and they were farming people. That meant they were always able to live with faith because the farmer always has something to look forward to—he plants his seeds. Depression happens when we don't have anything to live for. That's why farmers are believers in God—because they watch their seeds sprout and a new plant grow.

Wright
In 1955, with $500 in your pocket, you and your wife started a church. I understand that it took tremendous faith for both of you. What really impressed me, however, was the fact that you knocked on 3,500 doors to learn what the residents wanted—an enormous task. Do you believe that somewhere within the definition of faith lies a charge to do the work necessary for success?

Schuller
I had a whole year to do it. But, absolutely, that is the heart of what faith must be.

Wright

I've been a salesman most of my life. I'm in my sixties now, but I've been selling for years and years and anyone who does that much research and door knocking deserves to be successful.

You have referred to yourself as a "Christian Capitalist." Can you tell our readers what you mean?

Schuller

Well, I believe that people should try to achieve self-esteem and hopefully, independence. Freedom is the core of that. In the United States of America, we are free to achieve financial independence. It's not against the law as it would be in a pure socialist state or a pure communist state.

Capitalism is a principle of acquiring your own wealth. Capitalism is about the principles I find in Christianity that can be as bad as communism or anything else because it can generate greed, deception, theft, murder, you name it. Capitalism is very dangerous, just as freedom is very dangerous, without a set of personal morals and ethics. I say a Christian capitalist lives by three principles: (1) Earn all you can. Don't make it by trying to win the lottery—you have no pride of achievement if you go about it that way, (2) Invest all you can and, (3) Give all you can.

Wright

As I prepared for this interview, a prayer that you wrote titled "Success" struck me. In it you wrote this, *"Faith stimulates success. Hope sustains success. Love sanctifies success."* Would you comment on faith, hope, and love as it relates to your success?

Schuller

Well, nobody is going to be a true success, meaning satisfied with his accomplishments and living proud with the way that he did it, unless he lives by this trinity of faith, hope, and love.

Wright

Dr. Schuller, as a pastor of the largest RCA church, you were a part of the United States delegation to the funeral of the universally loved Mother Teresa in Calcutta. You stated that she was the "first lady of the twenty-first century." When did you first meet Mother Teresa and what impressed you the most about her faith in God?

Schuller

What I think impressed me most about her faith in God was that she was a happy person. She smiled. When I stepped off of the President's plane in Calcutta for the funeral, the first huge billboard we saw was her picture with the line, "Smile. It's the beginning of peace." I think I first met her through the writings of a now-deceased friend in England who became a Christian through her influence. More than thirty years ago I visited the Nirmal Hriday Home for the Dying that she founded in Calcutta.

Wright

The Crystal Cathedral is known worldwide as architectural excellence. Can you tell us about how it came to be and a little about its design?

Schuller

Yes. Well, I started this church, as you mentioned, with no money and couldn't find a hall to rent. I knew I had gifts because I was elected to Phi Beta Kappa in college, and national honor fraternities, so I knew I had talents and gifts, but I needed a place to speak. I couldn't find an empty hall anywhere.

Finally, I went to a drive-in theater and the guy there said that I could talk from the snack bar rooftop and that's how I started. That would be my church home for over five years. Every Sunday when I prayed or read the Bible or heard religious music, all I could see were clouds, the sky, trees bending in the wind, and birds flying. So, twenty years later when I needed a big church, I was homesick for the sky and said to the architect, "Why not make it out of all glass?" So, the Crystal Cathedral was born. It's where I came from as a child when I lived on the farm in the country and the sky was the most dominant thing.

Wright

When I was out at your church several years ago, I remember one of the guides there telling us something about the bricks. Instead of putting them horizontally, you had put them vertically. Is that true?

Schuller

It's not *really* true. It's true that Richard Neutra was my first architect and that's the one name I didn't see in your letter or your questions. Richard was probably the greatest architect for part of his life and he did the Tower of Hope and the cross on top of it. He did the Gallery and the first church that I had here. He said that he had always wanted to set stone vertically, but nobody would go along with it—but I did. So, the stone is set vertically here. It is a historic piece of architecture and we never use random stone, just the vertical stone. So, it's not bricks, it's stone.

Another thing that was missing in your questions was the last building we've built. It is the most glorious structure—I think it's outstanding. It was done by Richard Meier. The Getty Museum is doing the Pope's chapel in Rome. This is the only piece of real estate in the United States of America where the buildings are all done by gold medal, F.A.I.A. world-class architects: Richard Neutra's Tower of Hope, Phillip Johnson's Crystal Cathedral, and now Richard Meier's International Center for Possibility Thinking. We've gotten a lot of press on it and are going to get a lot more.

Wright

When I visited your church it was at Christmastime, I was fascinated by everything I saw. Some of my most cherished memories were of the sculptures on the grounds—the statues in the scene of the Pharisees and the adulterous woman spoke volumes to me. I didn't have to read the Bible to figure out what was going on. Can you tell our readers where all the beautiful art came from?

Schuller

It came from me. I've been in charge of this place for more than fifty years. Since I started with nothing, I have the principle that everything makes a statement—a weed says something, a flower says something, sidewalks make statements—everything makes a statement. I had Bible verses put in granite in the sidewalks so that people would just be walking and accidentally read a word from Scripture that might reach them. Then I chose to take what, in my life and heart, are the most important themes in the Bible and turn them into sculpture. *"Let Him who is without sin cast the first stone,"* that's the woman convicted of adultery (John 8:7). The prodigal son— you know the story?

Wright

Yes.

19

Schuller

Okay, so that's been done. The lost sheep story has been done. "Peace be still," is the title of the sculpture of Christ on the water. I picked what I call the most fundamental, historic, classical, powerful, and positive principles taught by Jesus and had them put in sculpture forms, all done by different sculptors. I've got, I think, seven different artists at work.

Wright

When you were talking a few minutes ago about earning as much as you can and investing as much as you can, what came to mind was the *Hour of Power* and all that you're able to do out there in Garden Grove—it just boggles the mind. I've been on a church staff for more than forty years and I just can't imagine how much all of that would cost weekly for you to be able to reach the entire world as you do.

Schuller

Well, we're on a sixty-five million dollar budget.

Wright

Wow!

Schuller

The income is always challenging. We've never had a surplus. If we had a surplus, we'd put it into expanding the business. What staff are you on?

Wright

I've been directing church choral music and I write choral music. Right now, I direct at the United Methodist Church here in Sevierville, Tennessee.

Schuller

Well, we've got a good choral conductor here.

Wright

I know. I listen all the time.

Schuller

I think he's the best.

Wright

He very well could be.

Schuller

The director of the Mormon Tabernacle Choir came to church here last week and said to our director, "Boy, we would like to sing in that cathedral."

Wright

Well, as a matter of fact, while I was waiting for you to come to the phone, your secretary put me on hold. I got to hear your choir sing for a minute or two.

Dr. Schuller, your *Hour of Power* reaches more than twenty million viewers weekly all over the world. You have the opportunity to have some of the most famous people in the world as guests at your church. Do your permanent members feel that they are really a part of a church that fills the need of your community and do they feel a closeness to each other?

Schuller

Not the way they should and that's why we had to open a new facility—the building we just opened. It cost me forty million, it took seventeen years, and you've never seen anything like it. Nobody in church work has ever built anything like it. The front of it opens wide so that when you are in the courtyard, instead of looking at a back wall with power poles and houses over the fence, you're looking at the front of a gorgeous building. The wall totally opens up and you see the huge living room. It's like the lobby of a five-star hotel. There's a beautiful food court, which is just shocking in its beauty. So, it's a gathering place for the people and it's doing wonders.

The congregation's attitude towards the *Hour of Power* is that they're assistant ministers. They meet the tourists who come here—a million a year. They sing in the choir for the *Hour of Power*. So, they feel a part of the community when they become a part of the four hundred hospitality people. They feel a part of the community when they join the music in the church. They're a part of the community when they man the phones for the twenty-four-hour New Hope Crisis Counseling Center—the first suicide prevention and telephone counseling ministry in the United States of America. It was established on September 15, 1968. So, organizations that participate in the ministry form their own sense of community and that's the way it's got to be. We also have small groups. I don't know how many small groups we have, but they all look upon the local television ministry as our primary world missionary work, which it is.

Wright

But, there's still a feeling of community.

Schuller

Only if they get into a small group or become one of the 3,000 members who form these working ministry groups. If they just come, sit in the pew, and go home, no, they don't feel like part of a community.

Wright

So, when I called some time ago, you were out inspecting some of the new construction. Are you saying it's on the same location?

Schuller

Oh, it is on the same location.

Wright

So, it's adjacent to the Cathedral?

Schuller

Yes. The three buildings form a triangle. The new building is reflected in the mirrored Cathedral and it can be viewed from the Tower of Hope. If you go through the new building, it is a museum that motivates. In architecture, the most important thing is the view. We don't have a mountain or a lake or a river view here, but what we've got is a view of two buildings that are world-famed for the art of their architecture. Those two buildings are the stunning view from the new building. Nobody has ever seen it until now because there were houses, power poles, and telephone poles. The west sides of the buildings are the most beautiful and now they're seen for the first time.

Wright

I just can't wait to see it.

Schuller

You would never know the place. It is stunning. We won first prize for the State of California for the landscaped gardens.

Wright

I came to Anaheim one time to do a speech on presentation skills for professional speakers and I drove to the Cathedral. It was at Christmastime and angels were flying around in the air—I couldn't believe it—and the orchestra was great. You are just so fortunate to have so much to work with there.

Schuller

I tell you, I am. I've been so fortunate to get the best people in the world to become my friends and they make it great; like Mary Martin, did you ever hear of her?

Wright

Oh, yes.

Schuller

Mary Martin was on the cover of *Life Magazine* seven times. She flew as Peter Pan. When I was putting together *The Glory of Christmas*, she said that I should have angels and they should fly. She said she knew how to do that and she took charge of it. She got the guy in here to make it happen and that's why we were the first church with flying angels.

Wright

I had no idea. Of course, Mary Martin and people like Ethel Merman are the grand ladies of Broadway.

Schuller

She's dead now, of course.

Wright

Yes. Dr. Schuller, you have acknowledged that the Rev. Dr. Norman Vincent Peale was one of your mentors.

Schuller

He was a pastor of our first church in America. Fifty-four Dutch colonists who bought the land from the Indians founded it in 1628.

We are the oldest corporation with an unbroken ministry in the United States, secular or sacred.

Wright

What do you think makes a great mentor? In other words, are there characteristics that mentors seem to have in common?

Schuller

First of all, it's excellence. They excel in their chosen career or field. That's the number one thing. Number two, they have to respect and love someone who they think has talent and possibilities. When you've got those two going, then you're on your way.

Wright

If you could have a platform, Dr. Schuller, and give our readers advice on how to develop their faith in God in order to live a richer, fuller, more meaningful life, what would you say?

Schuller

I would tell them that the most important thing is to believe in the cosmic being the Bible calls God. This God is personal, meaning He can think. He's not just a cosmic force or nothing to be admired at all. You can't admire electricity—you can be thankful for it, but you can't admire it. So God is intelligent, He is affectionate, and He is eternal. He is part of eternity.

The question is then how to develop an awareness of who He is and what He is like. The answer I give is: Jesus Christ. That's why Jesus Christ is the heart of my faith. Whether you are Protestant, Catholic, Jewish, or Muslim, He believes in God. That's why I believe in God. How do I know I'm right? I cannot believe that Jesus Christ was wrong. No way. If I think that I'm smarter than Jesus was when it comes to things like prayer and faith in God, then I'm the world's worst egotist and the most lacking in humility.

I think I'm living by Jesus' teachings and His claim to be the Son of God—the Savior. I'm living by it. I tell you, I was born in 1926 and I've had a fabulous life. I just look around and see what we've done here. I know that it has all come from God and from Jesus.

Wright

I certainly can see the fruits of His labor every time I look at the television and see that beautiful edifice there that just really reaches people all over the world. I really appreciate the time you have taken with us today. I wish you continued success, of course, in leading people to Christ. I think that you are just one of the great men of God.

Schuller

Thank you very much.

About The Author

In 1992, Dr. Schuller fulfilled one of his lifelong dreams with the opening of the Fuqua International School of Christian Communications, funded by the generous donation of Mr. J. B. Fuqua, of Atlanta, Georgia. Dr. Schuller serves as Chancellor of the school, where ministers from all over the world hone their preaching skills.

Dr. Schuller is the author of over thirty books, six of which have found a place on the *New York Times* and *Publishers Weekly* bestseller lists. Robert and Arvella Schuller have five children, all active in Christian ministry. Dr. Schuller's son Robert A. Schuller is also an ordained minister of the Reformed Church in America.

Chapter 3

BARBARA DWYER

David E. Wright (Wright)

Today we are talking with Barbara B. Dwyer, MSW (Master Social Worker). She is the founder and president of The BEE Attitudes, Inc., a company dedicated to building up men, women, and teens in secular and faith-based organizations by helping them embrace their God-given purpose, achieve their personal best, and strengthen their faith.

Her popular program, *The Art of Bee-Ing: Nature's Perfect Life Plan©,* is touching lives across the country. Barbara uses her passion for Christ and heart for people to make a bold and lasting difference in the lives of others. She has co-founded two highly acclaimed social service agencies: The Greater DuPage MYM, which provides services to teen mothers and The Community Career Center, which helps the unemployed. She is widely recognized as an influential business leader and advocate.

Barbara, welcome to *Speaking of Faith!*

Barbara Dwyer (Dwyer)

David, thank you, I am pleased to be part of this series.

Wright

You do a great deal of work helping people understand the importance of mental attitude. Do you see an interaction between faith and attitude?

Dwyer

Yes, indeed I do. To begin with, both attitude and faith are choices and each influences the other. Let me explain. A woman I've known all my life was raised in an affluent family. She graduated from college and got married. Her husband was a handsome charismatic man with great potential but he chose to squander it on booze, gambling, and loose women. After he lost her inheritance at a Las Vegas blackjack table—just after their third child was born—she divorced him. He skipped town never to return.

Unemployed and raising three children she had every reason to succumb to a bad attitude filled with resentment and anger. Rather than give in to that poison she chose to embrace her faith and develop an attitude of hope and possibility. She managed from paycheck to paycheck for fifteen years until she was stricken with breast cancer and underwent a radical mastectomy.

Undaunted, she held tight to her faith and the promise that God was always with her, and that He would bring her through this crisis too. Now, thirty years later my mother continues to be an example of faith in action. She re-married a few years after her surgery and celebrated her twenty-seventh wedding anniversary in 2005.

As a child in this family I learned firsthand the importance of believing—believing in a God who never loses sight of us, who listens to and answers prayers. If faith is believing what I haven't seen, then I am forced to rethink what faith really means, because I have seen too many miracles to believe in anything less than a very real and loving Savior.

Wright

So, what kind of miracles?

Dwyer

There have been many, David—physical, spiritual, emotional, and psychological. One of my favorite "God stories" comes from a time when I was twenty years old. It was a Saturday afternoon and I was home alone. My friend was coming over to pick me up and go out in two hours. I had just enough time to clean the kitchen, run the dishwasher and, get ready. I filled the portable, top-loading dishwasher, added the detergent, attached the faucet hose, and locked the lid. I was right on schedule. Unbeknownst to me a glass had broken and pieces of it had settled in the seam of the control panel. Leaning over to set the dial, the washer fan began to blow and shot pieces of broken glass into my eye.

I jerked my head back, fumbled to disconnect the faucet hose, and ran water over my eye to flush out whatever was imbedded. It didn't help. I tried it again. Nothing. With every blink the pain was intense. What should I do? Cell phones had were not being used yet so I had no way of contacting anyone. Looking at the clock through my uncut eye I realized my friend would be arriving in about half an hour so I went into my bedroom to pray.

At first I thought, "Okay, what's the lesson here? An eye for an eye?" No, that didn't make sense to me. So I offered God my fear and my hope. "Dear Lord," I prayed, "I don't know what's going on, but I'm scared. I don't want to lose the sight in my eye. I know you are here with me so I won't panic, but please let Terry [my friend] get here soon. Whatever the outcome is I will accept it, but I would really rather keep my sight. Let your will be done."

I waited. Terry showed up ten minutes early and took me to the emergency room. The hospital staff admitted me right away. A doctor administered an anesthetic to relieve the pain and after concluding his exam he determined I had successfully removed the glass, but he said my eye was badly cut. The anesthetic would wear off in two to three hours and the pain would return. With little more than a patch on my eye, a few aspirin and an appointment to see my ophthalmologist first thing the next morning, I went home to wait for the pain to return.

Two hours passed. Three hours passed. Five hours passed and the pain did not return. I just kept saying, "Thank you God." When I woke up the next morning there was still no pain. In the ophthalmologist's office the doctor read the Emergency Room report, carefully removed the patch, and examined the entire surface of my eye. He read the report again. Then, looked at my eye again. That made me a little nervous (no, a *lot* nervous). Uh-oh, what does this mean? He looked at my other eye. Then stepping back he crossed his arms, leaned on his desk and said, "I don't see anything wrong."

The miracle doesn't end there. I was given a vision test and saw everything with 20/20 clarity for the first time in ten years. Not only were the cuts completely healed, so was my nearsightedness—no more glasses!

Wright

That's an amazing story. So the doctor wasn't able to give you a medical reason for the change in your vision or the healing of your eye?

Dwyer

Nope; but I know what happened. God is very real to me. I chose faith.

Wright

We are taught that faith is called a spiritual gift, how can you call it a choice?

Dwyer

The choice is being open to receiving it. This spiritual gift of faith is like any other gift you might be given. Unless you receive it, you can't claim it. Think about what happens in homes across the world every year at Christmas. Paper is torn, ribbons are broken, and presents are opened with great excitement for what is inside. But what happens if a gift is never opened, or not appreciated and left to simply gather dust in the corner of the closet? Eventually, it is considered useless. It becomes nothing more than clutter and discarded altogether.

If we aren't open to God's providence in our lives how can we embrace it? Here is another way of looking at this issue of choice. While competing in the high jump during junior high school I tore the ligaments in my knee. After ten weeks the full-leg plaster cast was removed and to my astonishment my leg had shrunk considerably.

"My leg shrank! What happened?" I asked the doctor.

"Well, Barb," he explained, "you haven't used your leg for ten weeks and the muscles began to atrophy. What that means is they shrank from lack of use. Follow the exercises I prescribe and in time your leg will regain its full strength and both your legs will match again."

I think of spiritual gifts in the same way I think of physical muscles, if you don't use them they will atrophy—become weak and useless. We must choose to exercise the gifts God has endowed in us. When a muscle has gone weak from lack of use, it can be rehabilitated and brought back to strength. The same is true for our spiritual gifts. Through use, even the weakest faith can and will strengthen.

We are told very clearly in Matthew 7:7–8, "Ask, and it will be given you; seek, and you will find; knock, and it will be opened to you. For every one who asks receives, and he who seeks finds, and to him who knocks it will be opened."

I believe if we pray for and choose to receive faith we must put it to good use.

Wright

How do you practice faith?

Dwyer

That's a great question David, because I see faith as a verb—an action word, a process. While many think of it as a noun—something you can actually possess—I think that idea diminishes the real essence of faith. Just as love can be considered an action word, so too must faith. An action can be practiced.

Applying faith is a life-long journey of discovery. Again, a journey is based on action and so is faith. When building faith I begin with prayer. Being centered on prayer is key to developing a trusting and faithful relationship with Christ. He wants us to be in fellowship with Him, and even more importantly He wants to be in fellowship with us.

When I operated the Comprehensive Counseling Center, Ltd. I worked with scores of men and women of every age who had very poor self-esteem. Many were also shy and socially withdrawn. They would buy self-help books by the dozen hoping the right words would heal their woundedness and their esteem would be suddenly restored.

But, you cannot learn self-esteem from reading a book any more than you can learn to swim in a classroom. Swimming requires getting in the water; self-esteem requires getting into life. Developing positive self-esteem is based on getting out there and interacting with others, trying new things, getting involved, being encouraged, and having success. When these positive experiences are missing, positive self-esteem is impossible to build.

Faith is also developed this way. Pray and act, pray and act. Now I am not advocating a reckless kind of prayer and action. Praying that God heals your high blood pressure and then sitting on the couch nightly eating potato chips is not the way this works. Rather, I suggest you pray first, then listen . . . hear . . . and act.

You see, prayer itself requires faith because without faith you are simply talking to yourself. When you are open to the possibility that God hears and responds, then you are open to growing your faith. It isn't so much the size of your faith that matters—it is the size of your God.

Paul says it best in Romans when he explains, "Faith comes from listening to this message of good news, the good news about Christ"— Romans 10:17.

Wright

So, let's go back to attitude, your company is called The BEE Attitudes, Ltd. Capital B, Capital E, Capital E, Inc. How did you choose that name?

Dwyer

That is another faith journey God took me on. The title of my company actually has four meanings: "BEE" stands for **B**alance, **E**mpower, **E**nlighten; that's one meaning. It is also a homophone with the Biblical *Beatitudes* ("homophones" are words which have the same sounds but have different meanings and has a different spelling). The title is based on a great deal of research applying biblical principles to the lifecycle of the honeybee. And finally, attitude is critical to developing and practicing faith.

Let me share another story with you.

My three dearest friends and I were lounging around on my patio one night. We were settled in for a long night of girl-talk—stories about the men in our lives, our jobs, our children, our pets, but mostly about ourselves.

None of us remembers how it really began but it started a journey we are still on. Jane, the hospitality "diva" in our group, decided we should have a symbol that represents our friendship—a symbol that would characterize our special closeness, our feminine nature, and of course the enduring support we give each other.

The first suggestion was the butterfly. It is a nice symbol of rebirth and new life, and pretty, but the image of Steve McQueen's famous tattoo wasn't working for us.

Some time later, when we got together for another outdoor gab-session, the ideas began again. Remembering a story I had heard many years before about how the bumblebee had been studied by biologists and aeronautic engineers and both concluded it should not be able to fly, I offered as our symbol, "the bumblebee."

"The bumblebee?" Tilting their heads, my friends looked at me curiously and laughed in unison.

I was ready to explain. Experts explain the impossibility of a bumblebee flying by pointing out that its body is too large and its wings too small to support flight. The bumblebee defies science and apparent logic, allowing the miracle to take place. The bumblebee doesn't let the obvious, or the opinions of others stop it—it flies!

Now that's attitude!

My fascination with bees had begun. Like a bee to honey, curiosity compelled me to read about entomology, the study of insects, and more specifically, the bumblebee. While studying, I was disturbed to learn bumblebees tend to be slow, dim-witted, and rather reclusive—attributes, even in an insect, I don't hold in high regard.

For what I hope are obvious reasons, my friends and I did not want to be associated with a symbol for being slow, dim-witted, or reclusive, so we embraced the singular bumblebee lesson on attitude and abandoned the rest.

I turned my search to other bee species and came across the common honeybee. This bug is worth knowing! As I read about the extraordinary habits, behaviors, and intelligence of these insects my affection for them grew and grew.

I studied this insect for almost two years. My friends and family kept asking me why I was doing this and my only answer was, "I'm not sure." But the truth was I really did know. In my heart I understood God was leading me to an important lesson. I kept looking, and after my research was concluded, I sat curled up on my office couch, surrounded by textbooks and reams of notes, ready to discover what God has known all along—honeybees do indeed have something deeply spiritual to teach us.

Throughout the ages, honeybees have been associated with hard work, harmony, and prosperity. The lessons I learned are quite biblical in nature, for here is what they teach us:

1. Bee-Yourself
2. Bee-Hold Your Purpose
3. Bee-Come the Solution
4. Bee-Long
5. Bee-Courageous
6. Bee-Willing to Rest
7. Bee-True to Your Dance
8. Bee-Planful About Tomorrow

The BEE Attitudes, Ltd., is all about living life with gusto! Faith and a positive attitude are tightly joined because faith actually promotes a positive attitude of hope. I help individuals, and secular and faith-based organizations build faith, lighten-up, and appreciate and achieve their purpose—their personal best.

Wright

Those are interesting lessons you learned from the bees. How do you see them as being spiritual?

Dwyer

These lessons, *The Art of Bee-Ing: Nature's Perfect Life Plan©*, are founded on biblical principles. Let me give you a few brief examples.

Bee-Yourself, may sound simple but few of us, David, succeed in this quest. There are so many people, values, situations, and false teachings that attract people away from who they really are and were created to be.

First and foremost we are children of God. The Lord knew us before we were formed in our mother's wombs. There is no question He made each of us unique. It is written, "For as we have many members in one body, and all members do not have the same function, so we, though many, are one body in Christ, and individually members one of another"—Romans 12:4. We are called to use the different gifts He specifically and deliberately gave to each of us. God simply asks us to become the person He created us to be—no more, no less.

Wright

Which brings us to the second lesson, *Bee-Hold Your Purpose*. Barb, the topic of purpose has become very popular lately. What else can be said about it?

Dwyer

The great evangelical preacher Billy Sunday said it best, "More people fail through lack of purpose than lack of talent."

One of the problems with modern thought is the notion of creating your own purpose. In the ever-demanding world of self-expression, finding your own "groove" has taken on gothic proportions. The trouble with that kind of seeking is that you end up in the same place you started—egocentrically stuck on yourself. This second lesson naturally follows the first because we are asked to take our unique gifts and apply them. But how?

Bee-Hold Your Purpose is a very intentional title. Bee-Hold implies a revelation, which is how a real God-inspired purpose is endowed. God has a plan for each of us and His plan is prepared in advance for us to carry out.

My purpose was revealed to me as a young girl but it didn't make any sense to me until I was a young adult. My grandmother read Bible stories to me. I loved Matthew 4:19, "Follow me and I will make you fishers of men." It seemed silly but it captured my imagination as a preschooler. Half a century later it still provides my life focus.

This is how it happened. "When I grow up I'm going to be an art teacher!" was my earliest declaration. My future was settled as early as first grade. My mother, the consummate encourager, praised every painting, PlayDoh sculpture or drawing I scratched out. Mom became a teacher so I thought I would be a teacher too, until I enrolled in our local junior college. After graduating from high school I was excited to get started in my career. One critical element emerged which derailed my career track—lack of talent. Bless my mother's heart for I'm not a talented artist. Compared to students at the middle school level I can hold my own—not college. So, I dropped out.

Some months later I stayed up late reading a book. In the morning, my bed was so warm and cozy I didn't want to go to church. It was cold, my Mom and my sisters were still asleep, which meant no one was going to church. I was going to blow it off too. However, a force stronger than my fatigue and love for my warm bed lifted me out of bed and off to my very conservative, Missouri Synod Lutheran church home. This was out of character for me because I love to linger in bed on Sunday mornings.

Our pastor was a deeply caring man of God. In many ways he continues to be my measure of a great pastor. Rich in content, his sermons rarely held my adolescent short attention span, except for this one cold and dreary Sunday morning when he stood before the congregation and admonished us for allowing reprehensible jail conditions to exist.

You see, Pastor Lueking had recently visited the son of a parishioner at the Cook County jail and was shocked at the conditions he saw. His was an upper class white suburban congregation whose suffering tended to be issues not related to gangs, crime, poverty, and discrimination. With passion and eloquence he spoke of "our" responsibility to social issues.

Wright,

So tell me, what book had you been reading?

Dwyer

Well, the book I had just finished the night before was *The Cross and the Switchblade* by Reverend Dave Wilkerson. Have you read it?

Wright

No.

Dwyer

It is a true account of Reverend Wilkerson's work with inner city gangs.

I was a nineteen-year-old art education dropout when my real purpose was revealed to me. My purpose galvanized my heart. I had no clue what shape this would take, but I understood the path I was on—*to touch the lives of people*, to become a "fisher of men." I changed my major and pursued a degree in social work.

Purpose is designed for each of us according to our talents and gifts. I have heard over the years, "I could never do what you do." Well, I thank God for accountants and financial planners; I could never do what they do. It's no accident we might be gifted in one way and not in another. If we all possessed the same talents and temperaments this world would be very bland.

Wright

Are you saying that we each have been given one purpose in our lives?

Dwyer

No, I can't say we only have one. We are created as multi-dimensional beings and as such our purpose is more complicated. Christian scholars suggest a variety of ideas on the subject of purpose. I believe real purpose is unlikely to change over time, but how it plays out in life may change.

This is true in my life. For over two decades God's desire for me was to become a professional speaker. Like Moses, I disagreed with His choice, I argued that He had chosen the wrong person, and suggested He tap someone else for the job. Patient as always, God continued to nudge me until I could no longer turn a deaf ear.

The BEE Attitudes launched me into a whole new industry and ministry, but my life's mission hasn't changed. I'm taking His message as far and wide as He wants. He's the only reason my comfort zone has moved from addressing very small groups to filled auditoriums.

Wright

We don't have time to address all eight Lessons from *The Art of Bee-Ing: Nature's Perfect Life Plan©*, but will you give us an idea of what else you discovered?

Dwyer

Bee-Come the Solution directs us to ask questions. The power of asking questions is seen with most of Jesus' interactions with people. When we start asking questions and start listening to the answers, we start learning. The story of the Good Samaritan is one of the best examples of the power of a question. It begins with a question, "Who is my neighbor?" and ends with the answer, "How can I be a neighbor?" It takes a problem and redirects it to find a solution.

Let me relate this to bees. Bees have a problem—how to survive. In the summer when the temperature of the hive gets too hot the bees cannot survive. When this happens they go out in search of a solution. Forager bees go out from the hive in search of water rather than nectar or pollen. They return to the hive with their pollen pouches filled with water and deposit the water into the hive. They fan the water with their wings to quicken evaporation, cooling the hive.

Bee-Long beckons us to embrace God's plan to be in fellowship with each other. Let's face it—we are pack animals. We were not created to live in isolation. Just as the disciples were called to meet regularly for prayer, sharing meals and enjoying friendship, we too are expected to be in community as part of God's master plan for His people.

The old "Protestant work ethic" was one of my family's strongest values. Just pull yourself up by your bootstraps and keep going. This flies in the face of the importance of community. To understand the natural order of a Christian life is to understand the importance of being in relationship with others and the folly of trying to serve as our own god.

Wright

That's a bold statement, Barb. What would you say to someone who calls himself a loner?

I like that question, David. Having a sense of belonging doesn't require someone to be an extrovert or the life of the party. It simply means being connected to something meaningful outside of yourself. Quiet, solitary people may connect in a more subtle way, but connect they must. From the writings of King Solomon to the wistful sighs of Winnie the Pooh, "two are better than one."

This leads to the next lesson *Bee-Courageous*. "I am with you" is a common theme in the Bible. The firm knowledge that God will not forsake me gives me courage. As I shared with you earlier God called me into ministry before I was twenty. There was one element of the ministry I resisted—public speaking. I suffered from terrible anticipatory stage fright.

Moses' story, as I said earlier, is in many ways my story too. He was a reluctant speaker. He argued with God to appoint his brother who was quicker and more eloquent. I argued with God for twenty years, avoiding the stage whenever possible. But I continued to hear God's spirit voice calling me to speak. I simply couldn't shake it. When He gave me The BEE Attitudes I could no longer deny this gift. I had to face up to the fact that my fear was causing me to be disobedient to God's calling in my life.

It took a great deal of courage to fight the fear. But this affliction reminds me daily to line up behind Jesus and remember that He always walks one step ahead of me securing the path. What a relief!

Wright

What a relief indeed. Summarize the last three lessons for our readers, Barbara.

Dwyer

Bee-True to Your Dance helps people embrace the true rhythm of their lives. Too often we allow the tempo and style of our lives to be dictated by forces in the world. Dance requires balance, rhythm, concentration, and steps. In looking at my true dance I am aware of my tendency to lead and not follow. When I acknowledge that Jesus is the King of the Dance my pace becomes steadier and I allow myself to fall into step with Him. He never steps on my toes or loses the beat.

Bee-Willing to Rest is self-explanatory with one exception—the word "willing" is key! Willingness comes from the heart, which is where real change and healing takes place. It is essential to first become willing to do something before you ever do it. If I am not willing to pray regularly I'm not going to do it. If I'm not willing to go to the gym I'm not going to do it. If I'm not first willing to rest, I will not make rest a priority. Rest is essential to balance and health so I must acknowledge its importance and be willing to take the action.

And finally, *Bee-Planful About the Future* caps the lessons. I have been given my marching orders, I will follow my Lord and act on the words He has embedded in my heart, "Follow me and I will make you fishers of men." To Bee-Planful About the Future is to make a conscious effort to think about, set priorities for, and take action to accomplish the desires of God's heart.

Every area of life needs a plan. Whether it's a financial plan or a spiritual plan, we must understand that what we decide today will affect the future, giving credence to the importance of not ignoring tomorrow.

We all leave a legacy. For the most part I can determine what I leave behind. Through the memories I create, the actions I take, the people I touch, the assistance I give, and the words I speak, my legacy is being created. How will I be remembered? I can only hope. My greatest desire is when all is said and done, to hear, "Well done good and faithful servant."

Wright

What an interesting conversation. You know, when I tell my wife all these things you've taught me today about bees she's going to be fascinated. I really appreciate the time you've taken with me today, Barbara, it's been very, very interesting and I know it's been interesting for our readers.

Today we have been talking with Barbara Dwyer. Her company is dedicated to building individuals and teams by helping them embrace their God-given purpose, achieve their personal best, and strengthen their faith. Her popular program, the *Art of Bee-Ing: Nature's Perfect Life Plan©* is, as we have found out this afternoon, extremely interesting.

Thank you so much Barbara, for being with us today on *Speaking of Faith*.

Dwyer

David, it's been my pleasure and I thank you for the opportunity to share my faith journey.

About The Author

BARBARA DWYER, founder of the BEE Attitudes (Balance, Empower, Enlighten) created this program to help people appreciate and achieve their God-given talents and purpose. Barb's message transforms lives and organizations by contributing to the development of human potential, healing relationships and strengthening faith.

Barbara Dwyer, MSW is also Director of Community Development at Benedictine University in Lisle, Illinois. She is an award-winning leader and community-builder.

Barb is also a popular keynote speaker, seminar leader, author, and human potential expert who has presented to, universities, civic, religious, social groups and Fortune 100 companies. Known for her engaging warmth and enthusiasm coupled with twenty-five years of experience she inspires audiences.

Humor and honesty are the trademarks of Barb's work. Courageous enough to share personal stories of success and failure she uses her experiences to illustrate faith in action.

Barb is married to Tom and—depending on how you count—is the mother of three. She enjoys time with her family, her LIFT Group (Living In Faith Together), cats Wrigley and Oscar, Gigi the turtle, mid-life, gardening, photography, and volunteering for the American Red Cross.

Barbara travels from Chicago, Illinois.

Barbara B. Dwyer, MSW
President & Founder
The BEE Attitudes, Ltd.
Phone: 630.829.6003
E-mail: bdwyer@ben.edu
www.BarbaraDwyer.com

Chapter 4

DR. J. DAVID FORD

THE INTERVIEW

David Wright (Wright)

Today I am visiting with Dr. J. David Ford who has been involved in ministry since the early age of five. He comes from a long line of ministers. In fact, going back to 1705, for the past eight generations, except for one, all the men, from father to grandfather, etc., were ministers. The Ford family could very well be the most ministry-oriented family in American history. But, needless to say, Dr. Ford hasn't rested on the laurels of these past family ministers. Since he became president of the Evangelistic Messengers' Association in 1987 he has taken the ministry his father, Rev. O. L. Ford, co-founded in 1933, into over fifty nations.

Dr. Ford is also president of three other ministries which he has founded: More Than Conquerors School of Theology, New Hope Children's Foundation, and The Truth Shall Make You Free Ministries. Besides being involved in ministry across the U.S., since 1970 Dr. Ford has ministered the Gospel of Jesus Christ in numerous other countries.

Dr. Ford, welcome to *Speaking of Faith*.

Dr. J. David Ford (Ford)

Thank you, David. It's an honor to be with you.

Wright

Let me begin by asking you a personal question about your early ministry. Exactly how were you involved in ministry when you were only a child?

Ford

I started preaching when I was only five. My father would have me minister with him on the radio, as well as the revivals he was ministering in. Then, very often, Dad would just stop along the street, lift me up and set me on a park bench, or whatever was near, and tell me to preach. And preach I did!

Wright

That's amazing!

Ford

I don't know if my messages were theologically sound or not. But I preached so loud and so hard, I don't believe anyone had any trouble hearing me.

Wright

And now, some fifty years later, you are president of four international ministries. Please tell our readers something about them.

Ford

Let's talk about the oldest ministry first. My father, O. L. Ford, co-founded the Evangelistic Messengers' Association in Chicago in 1933. The E.M.A. was founded for the purpose of providing ministerial credentials for independent ministers. As far as we know, it's the oldest "nondenominational" or "interdenominational" ministry in the world. Since its beginning in 1933, E.M.A. has provided ministerial credentials for thousands of independent ministers in more than fifty countries of the world. Needless to say, we are still going strong today.

Wright

What about More Than Conquerors School of Theology?

Ford

I felt moved to establish MTC in 1992 in the Cleveland, Tennessee area. MTC was founded especially for those who had a real desire to study God's Word for the purpose of applying it to their lives. I call this "practical theology." Since that time we have moved MTC to Portage, Indiana. MTC not only provides a degree program here in the U.S. for students who take the courses "live," but for correspondent students as well. We also have what we call a "Fast Track Program." This is for those who are already working in leadership positions in ministries.

We have translated courses into Romanian and Spanish. We also have the first Bible school courses to ever be translated into the Miskito language for the Miskito Indian pastors who attend our extension schools. The Miskito Indians live in one of the most remote areas of Central America. Coupling our leadership training materials from MTC with pastors' conferences and MTC satellite schools, I have personally helped to train thousands of pastors.

Wright

That sounds exciting!

Ford

Yes, it is. It's also amazing. And it's all the Lord's doing!

Wright

And then you also direct New Hope Children's Foundation and The Truth Shall Make You Free Ministries.

Ford

Yes. In 2003, after seeing the tremendous need in Nicaragua, my wife Rose and I established the ministry of New Hope Children's Foundation. We just felt we had to do something to help feed, educate, and provide spiritual training for these children who are in such desperate need.

New Hope's Central American headquarters is located in the mountain village of El Crucero, which is about twenty-five miles from Managua. We have a school there where we provide a free, Christ-centered education for over 500 destitute children. If New Hope was not there, many of these same children could not otherwise afford an education. We also are operating New Hope Feeding Centers where we share the Gospel on a regular basis. We are presently feeding around fifteen hundred children. We are so blessed to have input into so many precious lives. Incidentally, we just opened an orphanage for Miskito Indian children in the most remote area of Nicaragua. And we do have a real need for volunteer staff workers in Nicaragua at several of our New Hope locations.

Wright

Maybe some of our readers will volunteer.

Ford

I hope so. And then The Truth Shall Make You Free Ministries is my personal ministry outreach where I minister the Word of God through radio, the printed page, the Internet, speaking engagements, conferences, etc.

Wright

I know my schedule is hectic; yours may even be more so.

Ford

Sometimes I feel like I am on a runaway train! It is just by God's grace that I am able to somehow keep up with it all.

Wright

I am sure you have had many obstacles to overcome in your thirty-five plus years of ministry. To what do you contribute your success?

Ford

If there is any success, it's purely God's mercy and grace, and the unshakable faith I have in the power of God's Word. I believe that I, as well as the ministries the Lord has entrusted to me, experienced a breakthrough after I began to understand more about the "working of faith" in my life. As my understanding was opened concerning this, it not only opened doors for me to walk through, but it also thrust me into a new spiritual dimension.

Wright

You mentioned "the working of faith." There has been a lot of teaching on faith, is there anything different about what you are saying?

Ford

I am not talking about "teaching on faith." I am talking about "the dynamics" behind the scenes of faith. What makes faith work? What drives faith? Why does faith always work? When I began to understand a few of these truths from God's Word concerning faith—this is "information"—I was in a better position to have these truths change my life. This is "application." God is far more interested in working "in" our lives, than He is in working "through" our lives. However, without "information," we will never progress to "application."

This is clearly seen in four steps in the Scriptures. First, there is the "hearing" of the Word. We read about this in Mark 4:24 and in Acts 10:44. Secondly, there is the "receiving" of the Word. We read this in Mark 4:20; Acts 17:11; and First Thessalonians 1:6 and 2:13. So first is the hearing of the Word. Then there is the receiving of the Word. And then what?

Wright

That's a good question.

Ford

Step three, the "understanding" of the Word. We see this in Matthew 13:19 and 23. Now we are ready for step four: the "keeping" of the Word. This is found in Luke 8:15. How do we keep it? Jesus said in Luke 11:28 that those who hear the Word and keep it are blessed. How do we keep the Word?

Wright

I'm listening.

Ford

By "doing" it! Jesus said in Luke 8:21 that His mother, brothers, and sisters were those believers who hear the Word of God and do it. First John 2:5 informs us that if we "keep" the Word of God, the love of God is perfected in us. How do we "keep" it? By doing it. James 1:22 says that we are to be "doers of the Word" and not hearers only or we are deceiving ourselves. (You will have to pardon me, David, I get kind of excited and caught up in this when I think about what activates the power of God's Word in our lives.)

Wright

That's perfectly all right.

Ford

Having said this, and hopefully we now understand these spiritual principles, we are ready to take the next step in understanding more about faith.

Wright

I'm ready!

Ford

Christ said in Matthew 17:20 that if we have faith as a grain of mustard seed, we can speak to a mountain and it will move. Christ reinforced this in Luke 17:6 when he said if we have faith as a grain of mustard seed, we can speak to a tree and it will be removed. Often teachers teach on the importance of words and how we are able to speak words in faith that will produce results. That's good. But I believe it's also good to understand the "workings of faith." If we don't understand *why* faith is able to work in our lives and produce results, we may not have the confidence we need to preserve when we are facing some of the critical situations we will all face in life at one time or another.

Wright

You are getting me interested, go on.

Ford

Jesus said in Mark 4:30–32 that the kingdom of God is like a grain of mustard seed, which, though it is less than all the seeds of the earth, after it is sown, it grows and becomes greater than all the herbs. The Bible says it develops great branches, so great that even birds come and lodge under its shadow.

We learn from this that although the mustard plant starts as a seed, it doesn't remain a seed. If, and I say, "if" the mustard seed receives nourishment and the right conditions, it undergoes a phenomenal transformation from seed to tree. The more we understand what is involved in that transformation, the better we will understand the "power of faith" and how it can become a deciding factor or force in our lives.

Wright

The mustard seed is a very small seed, isn't it?

Ford

Yes, one of the smallest. If you were to hold just one mustard seed in your hand, you would hardly know it was there. It could be compared to about the size of the point of a pencil. But if the conditions are right, it doesn't stay that way. What will happen to the seed if the conditions are right?

Wright

It grows.

Ford

And understanding the growth process helps us better understand faith—how it increases in our lives, how it works, and why it works.

There is power in a seed, isn't there? Regardless if it's a mustard seed or an oak seed, everything that is needed for that tree to one day materialize is in the seed. Though it is invisible to our naked eye, as we hold an oak seed in our hand and look at it, everything that seed needs to grow is there.

The trunk of the mighty oak is there. The oak leaves are there. The bark and the great roots that reach down into the earth are there. Everything that oak tree needs to reach up sixty feet into the sky is there inside that little seed. So it is with faith. Everything we need, just like the mustard seed or oak seed, is in the seed of faith. The measure of faith that Jesus talked about in Romans 12:3 is that faith that every man receives.

Wright

Okay, I am getting the picture. Faith starts in our lives like a seed—a mustard seed which is so tiny.

Ford

That's right. But it's also important for us to understand that though this "seed of faith" may be very small in our lives, like the mustard seed or other seeds; yet, this seed is supernatural. It is the very Word of God!

Jesus revealed this truth to us in the parable of the sower. In Luke 8:11 we learn that the seed is the Word of God. Now if the seed Christ imparts into our hearts and lives when we receive Him as our Lord and Savior is the very Word of God, as Jesus says it is, then the more we understand about a seed, the better we will understand the workings of the seed of the Word of God in our lives. Is that a fair statement?

Wright

Yes, it is.

Ford

Since the "natural" types the "spiritual," as we compare the "natural" with the "spiritual," we can better understand some of the "hows" and "whys" of the "working of faith" in our lives. And as "information"—even knowing just a few spiritual principles—gives way to "application," the faith Christ has planted in our hearts will be activated and produce phenomenal, life-changing results! Understanding some of the "hows" and "whys" of the working of faith in our lives, "enables us," or better put, "empowers us" and gives us the spiritual strength and spiritual fortitude to overcome the challenges we all face in life.

Wright

What are some of these spiritual principles?

Ford

First, we need to understand that if the conditions are right in our spiritual life, the seed of "faith" of God's Word will grow within us. In Acts 12:24, the Bible states that the Word of God grew. There is great power in the Word. Power! Power first of all to do what? Grow!

Faith isn't something we conjure up or produce on our own. Faith isn't a New Year's resolution. Faith isn't a mere confession. Hebrews 11:1 informs us that faith is a substance. It's real. Faith is something very real that God produces within us as we yield to Him and His Word. If we will allow, or better yet, nourish the seed of faith that every child of God has received, that faith will grow in our lives. Second Thessalonians 1:3 tells us that faith can grow in our lives. This Scripture also states that our faith can grow exceedingly.

The question before us now is, "How does faith grow?" What must happen in our lives before faith can grow to the point that it becomes "stronger" than any thing we may face in life?

Wright

Go on.

Ford

Okay! First, let's look at the natural. We know Jesus used natural, everyday occurrences and stories in his teaching, which we know as parables, to personify spiritual principles. So, let's take the mustard seed we have been talking about and get ready to plant it. But before we plant it, what do we need to do?

Wright

Prepare the soil.

Ford

Exactly! Before you can plant anything, the soil must be prepared for the planting. It's the same way with the seed of God's Word. God's Word cannot be planted in our lives until we have become a new creation in Him. In Second Corinthians 5:17, Paul stated that if we are in Christ, we are a new creation. That's what has to happen before the seed of the Word can be planted in our hearts. Paul goes on to say that old things have passed away in our lives and all things are now new. It's that new soil with all the old rocks of sin, stumps, and roots of the world taken out of our lives that puts us in a position to be able to receive the engrafted Word of God.

Now that our spiritual soil is prepared and ready, what is the first thing that has to happen to the mustard seed before it can grow?

Wright

I guess the seed has to die.

Ford

It's the very same in our lives. That is why the Apostle Paul said in First Corinthians 15:31, "I die daily." If the Word and faith is going to grow in our lives so we possess the power to overcome life's obstacles, we must die to our wants and our desires. Galatians 5:24 states that those who are Christ's have crucified the flesh with its affections and lusts. If we yield to the Word of God as it comes into our lives, the Word brings death to our "self-life." As our self-life is destroyed, it's progressive—our "faith life" will continue to grow within us.

Paul said in Romans 6:6 that our old man, or old nature, is crucified with Christ. That's part of the dying process that must take place to our old carnal life and carnal mind that are at enmity with God. We can only walk in the Spirit to the degree that our old nature has been subdued. Needless to say, this is an ongoing process. That's why

Paul said our old man "is" crucified. Notice, it's present tense. This is something that is continual. If we are going to "walk in the Spirit," this process has to continue until we go home to be with the Lord.

Now that we have gotten past dying to self, we are getting to the exciting part.

Wright

What is that?

Ford

The growing of the Word within us. As we "die to self," our old nature decreases—becomes smaller. Our new spiritual nature, our new man, becomes larger.

Wright

I never thought of it quite like that.

Ford

Let's go back to the mustard seed we planted. If it's going to grow, what must it have?

Wright

Moisture, water, sunshine.

Ford

Amen! So it is in the spiritual. The seed of the Word must be nourished within us. Just as in the natural, the conditions must be right if the seed is going to grow, so it is in the spiritual. We must provide the seed of faith that comes into our lives the right spiritual environment for it to grow. Maybe we can come back to this thought later. But first, let me share with your readers another spiritual principle on faith that has changed my life, both naturally and spiritually.

Acts 19:20 informs us that not only does the Word of God have the power to "grow" mightily, but it also has "power to prevail."

Now we are coming to the part that enables us to become a "victor" in life rather than just a "victim." It's the "prevailing power" of the Word that "enables us" to overcome the obstacles that come our way in life. Not only will the Word "grow" in our lives, but it will also "prevail." I believe the overcoming power that all of us can experience in our lives comes from the Word of the Lord. We do not receive this power to overcome just because we speak the right words. I believe it's far deeper than that!

Wright

What do you mean?

Ford

As it is in the natural, so it is in the spiritual. Remember that tiny, little mustard seed we planted a few minutes ago?

Wright

Yes.

Ford

It not only has the power to "grow," but it also has the power within it to "prevail." That is, if the conditions are right. The mustard seed, if it is to be successful and come to maturity, must also overcome the obstacles life throws at it—the hardness of the soil, or the pebble, or rock, that has rolled on top of it. Have you ever seen a little tree growing in the crack of a sidewalk?

Wright

Yes.

Ford

What happened? Well, somehow, that seed—perhaps an acorn from a mighty oak—fell into that crack. What did the seed do? The same thing we have to do—make the best of a mess! The very thing God intended for it to do, the little seed began to grow. Not only did it grow, but it also "prevailed" over the concrete that surrounded it, hindering its growth. In fact we must go beyond that. The prevailing power that little seed had was greater than the power of the concrete. As the little seed grew it prevailed over the concrete by breaking it to pieces.

(I'm about to preach, David.)

Wright

Okay!

Ford

I remember when I was standing in front of one of the emperors' tombs in China. I looked up the wall and saw a sapling about the size of my arm growing. What had happened? The little tree had "grown" and "prevailed" over the stone of the emperor's tomb.

Wright

That must have been quite a sight.

Ford

Yes, it was. If a natural seed, say, a mustard seed, can grow and prevail over the circumstances it faces in life; how much more can the seed of God's Word grow in our lives and give us the necessary strength to prevail over the obstacles we face.

The Word of God has all the power we need to enable us to live as "conquerors" instead of the "conquered." The Word of God, when it comes into our lives, has both "growing" and "prevailing" power. These, I believe, are some of the keys to what faith "is" and "how it works."

Wright

You are giving us something to think about.

Ford

I believe that faith to overcome obstacles in life comes in stages. The more the mustard seed grows, the stronger it becomes and the more prevailing power it has to overcome whatever it may face. Faith is the same way.

Romans 12:3 states that God gives each of us a "measure of faith." What we do with our measure, or better yet, what we *allow* God to do in our lives with our measure of faith will be the deciding factor as to how much our faith grows.

In the Bible, when little David was challenged by a lion that had come to steal a little lamb from his sheepfold, David didn't back down. Later, when a big bear was blocking his pathway, no doubt, he thought back to how God had given him victory over the lion. This encouraged him not to back down from the bear.

Then when David heard the giant, Goliath, defying the armies of God, he was ready for the battle. Why? He told King Saul he had already been victorious over the lion and bear. David said to Saul, "The Lord that delivered me out of the paw of the lion, and out of the paw

of the bear, He will deliver me out of the hand of this Philistine."
What is this demonstrating?

Wright

How God can help you face anything.

Ford

That's true. But we also see here that David's faith had grown so
much from facing and conquering previous obstacles in his life, he
was now ready to take on this big, bad giant that no one else wanted
to fight.

Wright

Amazing!

Ford

I have seen this spiritual principle work in my life and ministry
over and over again. Since I am so deeply involved with missions and
world-evangelization, I'm thinking now of how understanding this
principle has helped me on the mission field.

I remember the first time I made a mission trip to the Ukraine. I
was due to hold a crusade in another city—a six-hour train ride from
where I was. But there was a catch. We could not secure return tickets. It seemed there were none available. And, I had to be back at a
certain time or the plane would leave for Moscow without me.

Wright

That was quite a predicament to be in.

Ford

It sure was. But I had walked with the Lord for years, and I had
seen His handiwork many times in the past. So I just knew He was
going to provide for our return train tickets.

Wright

What did you do?

Ford

My team members and I boarded the train by faith and went and
held the crusade. The night the crusade was over, God provided us

with return tickets. So we returned to our city of departure in time to board the plane to Moscow.

Wright

Wonderful!

Ford

Now let me tell you what happened about a year or so later. I took another team to Kiev, Ukraine, where I was due to speak at a Bible college. Then we were going to conduct a few crusades in several different cities. However, I felt God spoke to my heart that after I finished my lectures at the school, instead of conducting crusades, I was to take several of the team members and leave as soon as possible for the most western city in the Ukraine—the city of Uzgorod. This was not a six-hour train ride, but an *eighteen-hour* train ride. And this time, I could not even secure the tickets to go there, nor did we have hotel reservations in Uzgorod upon our arrival. The icing on the cake was that neither could we secure tickets for our return trip to Kiev.

Wright

That was even more of a predicament to be in.

Ford

Yes, it was. The truth is, I never would have gone on this eighteen-hour train ride if I had not seen God already provide on the six-hour train ride. Because, like David, I saw the hand of God providing for me in a smaller sense, so I was ready to move up to my "Goliath" without any fear or reservations.

Wright

What happened this time?

Ford

By faith, we went to the train station, packed and ready to go— believing we would be able to purchase tickets after we arrived at the station. God was faithful. We were able to purchase one-way tickets from a man we met in the train terminal. Now we could go to Uzgorod. However, we still had no return tickets. But that wasn't important. I knew that if God took care the first leg of our journey, He would take care of the rest of our journey.

Wright

What happened next?

Ford

We made the train trip to the city of Uzgorod without incident. We found a vacancy in a hotel, which was no small thing and made the contacts I felt we should make. Then, once again, when we were ready to go home, we were able to purchase return tickets from someone much in the same manner as we did when we went to Uzgorod.

Wright

I'm impressed.

Ford

So am I—in the Lord's provision. I have seen this over and over again in our ministry as well and in my wife Rose's and my personal lives. I wish I had time to share with you the many times God has moved for us and given us victory over the smaller obstacles we faced to prepare us for the giant obstacles we had to face in the future. God is so faithful—far more than we merit or deserve.

Wright

Yes, He is.

Ford

I believe this same principle is at work in many of your readers' lives and they may not even realize it. Sometimes we need to push the "pause button" on our lives so we can "wait on the Lord" and take a good look at what is going on in us. More than likely all of us have had the handwork of God manifested in our lives when we didn't even realize it. If we don't take the time to "wait on the Lord," we will fail to recognize that God is at work in our lives.

Wright

Amen!

Ford

Okay, so we learn from this that our past victories in life prepare us for our future victories. Isn't that great?

Wright

It sure is.

Ford

But it's also important for us to understand something else about this. Just as past victories prepare us for future victories, our past defeats can set the stage for future defeats.

Wright

I can see that too is true. What do people do if they have experienced many past defeats in their lives?

Ford

Paul told us in Philippians 3:13 that we must forget those things which are behind. If we are going to overcome the challenges life hands us, we must not dwell on past defeats. We have all had some victories. We must thank the Lord for those victories and meditate on them. As we do this, our past victories become our stepping-stones to future victories. Just as our past defeats—if we dwell on them—will become our stumbling stones to future defeats.

It's also important for us to understand that God prepares us in steps. It was no accident that a lion came looking for a lamb chop dinner among the sheep that David was watching. It was no accident that a bear also showed up on the scene to challenge David's faith process. God was preparing little David for the big battle that was to come. And, just as He prepares us, He was preparing David in steps.

There are those who may one day read these lines who need to understand that what they may be going through is because God is preparing them so they will be ready to meet tomorrow's challenges. If David had bit the dust on the challenge of the bear or lion, he would never have had the joy of having God use him to overcome that mean, nasty, old giant. If we "roll over and play dead" whenever we face a stray jackrabbit in our trail, we'll never know the sweet taste of winning the victory over the lion. The more difficult the battle, the sweeter the victory.

Wright

That's encouraging—especially if we are hearing these words in the midst of a battle.

Ford,

It sure is. It's also good to know that God never sends us in the wrong direction. We are facing today what we need to face so we will be ready for what we will have to face tomorrow. We must not be alarmed just because a lion is roaring at us or a bear is growling at us. If we are walking in God's will, He is going to bring us through it!

Wright

I believe that.

Ford

These two very simple spiritual principles I have shared today—the power of the Word in our lives to "grow" and "prevail"—can produce a new realm of faith in the lives of your readers, if they will only apply this to their lives.

No matter how often or how many times we have stumbled and fallen spiritually, God desires to turn yesterday's failures and defeats into today's victories. Whatever any of us are going through right now, we can rest assured, God is more than able.

For instance, if any of your readers are going through a financial difficulty now, they need to think back to a time when they didn't have the money to meet a need and God brought them through it. He will do it again. Regardless of the problems we are now facing, if we have walked with the Lord for some time, as we recount our past victories—not defeats—new faith will come alive within us!

Wright

Dr. Ford, you have certainly challenged my thinking. As we conclude this interview, what final thoughts do you have that could help those who are struggling with or have even been overcome by obstacles in their lives?

Ford

If we don't trust the Lord to give us strength and power through His Word to help us conquer the small things in our lives, how will we ever conquer the big things? We need to always remember that God never sends us in the wrong direction. Sometimes it's easy for us to think we are out of God's will because things are going wrong in our lives. I don't know how many people—even preachers—have missed God's best and quit, just because the going got tough. If you are sure you are in God's will, don't run off in fright just because a "lion" is roaring at you or a "bear" is blocking your path.

We need to also remember that God's timing is always right. If we are facing a particular obstacle or obstacles now, it means it is the right time in our lives for us to face it. God doesn't make mistakes. He ordains our battles. And, if we are going to fulfill the spiritual destiny God has for our lives, there is no way to escape the battle that is before us.

It's also good to know that a battle often comes before a promotion. All the men and women we read about who have been used greatly by God, continually had to overcome great obstacles—lions, bears, giants, financial problems, discouragement, sicknesses, and the list goes on and on. It wasn't by their own might or strength that they won the victory. It was the power of the Word working within them, giving them the needed faith and strength to overcome and prevail over their circumstances.

We all must meet life's giants one by one. We will either slay them or they will slay us.

David, I hope your readers will always remember that regardless of what comes their way, God will always make it work for their good. If someone is facing something right now that seemingly there is no way to go around it, over it, or under it; then with God's help and the power of His Word, they can go *through* it!

About the Author

Dr. J. DAVID FORD is president of four international ministries. Evangelistic Messengers' Association, a ministry to "independent" ministers, was founded by his father in 1933. E.M.A. provides ministerial credentials to ministers around the world, as well as 501(c)(3) tax-exemption for churches and ministries in America (www.emai.org). More Than Conquerors School of Theology and Bible Institute provides both classroom and correspondence training in "practical theology." MTC has a special "Fast Track Program" for leaders to help them earn their degree. MTC is both accredited and affordable (www.morethanconquerors.org). New Hope Children's Foundation is making a big difference in many of the lives of unfortunate children in Central America (www.newhopechildrensfoundation.org). The Truth Shall Make You Free Ministries publishes Dr. Ford's "tell it like it is" messages by printed page, audio, and on the Internet (www.thetruthshallmakeyoufree.org). To invite Dr. Ford to come and minister at your church, or for additional information on these "cutting-edge" ministries, visit Dr. Ford's web sites, or you may call or write him.

J. David Ford
Shekinah Lakes World Outreach Ministry Center
100 Charity Lane
Huntingdon, Tennessee 38344
Phone: 731.986.4450
Fax: 731.986.3620
E-mail: jdf@shekinah.com

Chapter 5

JANA ALCORN

David Wright (Wright)

Today we're talking with Jana Alcorn. Jana has been involved in worldwide humanitarian efforts, evangelism, and global leadership development. She is the founder of Dream Builders Network and Hayley's House, a house of hope and mentorship for orphaned and abandoned children in Arusha, Tanzania. She hosts her own television program and is also author of a growing number of books and articles. She travels as a camp meeting and conference speaker and is a strategist, life coach, and consultant. The Lord has called her to equip and encourage and evangelize. In obedience to that call, her ministry has touched over forty countries, fulfilling the Great Commission of Jesus Christ. She and her son, Jordan, live in North Alabama.

Jana, welcome to *Speaking of Faith*.

Jana Alcorn (Alcorn)

Thank you, David. It is great to be here to share what the Lord is doing and how people can overcome the challenging places of life and enter into their God-ordained destinies. The Holy Spirit has given me principles that are going to inspire so many to walk in their God-given destinies.

The storms of our lives are indicators.

In December of 2004 and in August of 2005, two similar disasters hit our world. The Asian Tsunami of that December day would be among the worst in the history of the world. The death toll climbed day after day as finally almost 250,000 souls were numbered as gone out into eternity. Some storms can come without warning. Leather-skinned fishermen were routinely slinging their home-made nets from small wooden boats; children were playing in the white sand of the beaches; young couples in love walked hand in hand, barefoot in the sands of one of the world's most beautiful paradises. Then it hit. Total confusion, panic, chaos, fright, flight, and madness followed—screams, yells, noises, sounds of agony. And then, after a while . . . silence. Indonesia and many parts of Asia will never be the same. Storms have a way of changing the landscape.

What should have been a normal day in August produced the worst natural disaster in our nation's history. Hurricane Katrina would be a fierce visitor that would leave its crisscrossed footprint upon the pristine South. The beautiful, historic New Orleans, Louisiana, suffered a direct hit. In less than twenty-four hours, one of the largest cities in the United States became a toxic soup bowl. Bodies floated, children were separated from parents; the sick and frail and elderly suffered beyond our ability to describe. The entire city was under a mandate of forced evacuation. Neighboring southern states were not spared. One storm can affect many, many people.

Wright

I know that you have firsthand experience in some of life's roughest weather. I understand that you and your son recently went through one of the deepest and darkest challenges of life that one could face. Today I am sure our readers would want to hear your story of overcoming. So why don't we just let you take your time and open your heart and speak to us as the Lord would inspire you to do so.

Alcorn

Thank you, David. You know, none of us can choose our storms, but we can choose our building materials. The Bible tells us that our foundation must be none other than Jesus Christ Himself.

I'd like to give everyone some practical, biblical guidelines to overcoming in the storms of life and I believe it is possible to overcome any storm of life.

Most everybody that you meet has encountered some kind of storm in life. It doesn't take a very long lifespan to begin to understand that there is more to our gift of time here than sunny days and cool breezes. The struggles of life and the pressures of life oftentimes do more to strengthen our faith in the Lord Jesus than the blessings of prosperity and smooth sailing.

God forges us in the furnaces of affliction. The wealth that comes with overcoming the storms of life distinguishes the sprinter from the long distance runner. Real runners run in the rain! And the rains will come.

Jesus once told a story about two houses. Both of them faced the wind, the rain, the floods, and the storm. However, one stood and one fell. What was the difference? What could make one continue to stand against onslaughts from without and flooding from within? The difference in the two houses was the foundation. A foundation cannot be seen by others and is one of the least attractive parts of the building. But when God begins to build us in Him in the early formative years, He places emphasis and time in the foundation of our lives. If you faced a tsunami of a storm today, would you stand? Could you overcome through horrific onslaughts? When everything shifts, will you still be upright in Him? With your firm foundation in Christ Jesus, our Lord, you will remain standing after the raging torrents of hell have mercilessly pounded against every realm of life.

- "According to the grace of God which is given unto me, as a wise master builder, I have laid the foundation, and another buildeth thereon. But let every man take heed how he buildeth thereupon. For other foundation can no man lay than that is laid, which is Jesus Christ."—I Corinthians 3:10–11

I know what it means to have your hopes and dreams dashed to the ground and for every circumstance of life to seem to loudly contradict the things you knew the Lord had told you. When your heart is so torn apart and the devastation has been so obvious that even friends and family wonder if you will ever overcome, it's time to keep looking to the Source of life.

The storms are not an indication of your lack of faith, but rather it is the very storms of life that prove and demonstrate our faith. When I am challenged by life, I am not trying to find someone with accolades and stars, but show me the person with the scars—the scars of weathering the storms of life and coming out with a praise in the heart. It is to that believer who respects the power of the storm to transform that God says, "The thunder of My voice will become the most dominant force of your life." I want all those who are braced for the storms of life to know that crisis and chaos can become the womb of your miracle!

There are many kinds of storms in life. There are six areas of your life that I can assure you will be tested in some form:

1. Spiritually,
2. Physically,
3. Relationally,
4. Mentally,
5. Financially,
6. And in your destiny.

Storms, storms, storms. It would be easy to believe that storms are the normal occurrences of even our everyday life. But don't believe it—they come, but they pass. And then the sun shines again. Even with all the storms of life, never develop a "storm mentality."

Wright

Since you just mentioned some of the various storms that we will all face, share with us some of the ways that God has led you through life's storms.

Alcorn

Our family's story is still difficult for me to talk about, but God has so given me an assignment of encouragement that He has provided me the grace to help others through their own storms, especially ones like the one we faced.

In January of 2005, all of our family members came down with terrible bad winter colds. I was sick, our eleven-year-old son was sick, my mom was sick, and my husband, Bill, was sick! We were just shut in from the weather, lying around the house, drinking cup after cup of chicken soup, and taking advantage of the time to enjoy extra family time, which we all loved doing anyway.

In February we all got better—all except Bill. And he just could not seem to shake this cold. Finally, in March he was hospitalized and the diagnosis was pneumonia. He was given antibiotics and sent home all well and good. Except it wasn't good. April was coming and with it some of the most crushing words a family could hear.

I remember when my husband and I sat crying on our living room couch, just after we had heard devastating words from our team of doctors. Bill was always the picture of strength and vitality. Now, our own personal "tsunami" was at our own door and everything in our lives was shaking. My darling husband and best friend in life, who had never used tobacco in any form, was now facing a diagnosis of lung cancer, advanced stages, inoperable, and aggressive. How could this be? We didn't fit the profile. We didn't do the "hospital thing." We were not "doctor" kind of people. Besides, our son, who was only eleven, needed both a mom *and* a dad! I can tell you firsthand that when your storm comes to this level of intensity, you will run to the Rock of Ages and cling to Him with all of your might!

This is when faith must graduate to trust. First of all, we trust the Lord for Divine healing based upon the finished work of Christ:

- "Surely he hath borne our griefs, and carried our sorrows: yet we did esteem him stricken, smitten of God, and afflicted. But he was wounded for our transgressions, he was bruised for our iniquities: the chastisement of our peace was upon him; and with his stripes we are healed."—Isaiah 53:4

But if that healing doesn't manifest as quickly or in the way we think it should, then we should trust God in the face of adversity.

- "In the Lord put I my trust . . ."— Psalm 11:1
- "What time I am afraid, I will trust in thee."—Psalm 56:3

A wind is something we cannot control. That does not mean we sit passively by as Christians and not be proactive in the manifestation of God's promises. It just simply means that there are currents of life wherein we must simply trust Him when we can't trace Him.

There are two things God will always teach us: (1) His Word, and (2) His ways. And He has promised us:

- "When thou passest through the waters, I will be with thee . . ."—Isaiah 43:2

We have to know that He is with us and that He is always working all things for our good if we continually lean on and rely upon Him

- "And we know that all things work together for good to them that love God, to them who are the called according to his purpose."—Romans 8:28

Wright

Jana, what happens when it seems like the word God has given to us will never come to pass? What about those times when it seems that God has forgotten us?

Alcorn

David, that brings us to another storm. The storm of promises delayed. But we all have to learn that delay is not denial. I have actually found that when a promise is delayed, there is a reason. I may not know the reason or even understand, but God is working a far greater plan than we can see.

The Word of God is a storehouse of examples of men and women, and even children, who overcame the storms of life. Abraham, the patriarch of the nation of Israel, endured through the storm of a promise delayed. Abraham waited almost twenty-five years for the birth of his promised son Isaac. Not only did he father a son—he fathered a nation! Perhaps your promise has been delayed; continue to trust God until the storm passes by. Like Abraham, there is more in you than what you know.

- "(As it is written, I have made thee a father of many nations,) before him whom he believed, even God, who quickeneth the dead, and calleth those things which be not as though they were. Who against hope believed in hope, that he might become the father of many nations, according to that which was spoken, so shall thy seed be. And being not weak in faith, he considered not his own body now dead, when he was about an hundred years old, neither yet the deadness of Sara's womb: He staggered not at the promise of God through unbelief; but was strong in faith, giving glory to God; And being fully persuaded that, what he had promised, he was able also to perform."—Romans 4:17–21

I think one of the greatest success keys in life is learning to persevere. The Apostle Paul never said I quit, but he did say, "I have finished my course . . ." Jesus, while on the cross, never said, "I quit," but He did say, "It is finished."

I like Matthew 24:13 in *The Message* version of the Bible:

- "Staying with it—that's what God requires. Stay with it to the end. You won't be sorry . . ."

Wright

So, God really does expect us to keep on keeping on, doesn't He? What are some keys you have used in your personal life when God's promises were delayed?

Alcorn

David, yes, God does expect us to persevere and to persevere in faith. Two of the essential keys to this are: the right mental attitude and the right kind of self-talk. Your attitude reflects your altitude. Proverbs 23:7 tells us:

- "For as he thinketh, in his heart, so is he . . ."

Every thought that comes into your mind doesn't belong to you. Other people can give you thoughts by what they say. The devil can put thoughts into your mind. They only become yours when you extend an invitation and put out special couches for them to sit on.

In 2 Corinthians 10:5 Paul writes that we are to take every thought captive:

- "Casting down the imaginations, and every high thing that exalteth itself against the knowledge of God, and bringing into captivity every thought to the obedience of Christ . . ."—2 Corinthians 10:5

In other words, God has a way of helping us overcome in our thought life.

Satan attacks our peace by attacking our thought life. Philippians 4:7 says that the peace of God will stand as a garrison and guard and protect our heart:

- "And the peace of God, which passeth all understanding, shall keep your hearts and minds through Christ Jesus."—Philippians 4:7

If your peace is being attacked today, it is because it is the soldier that is guarding the gateway of our lives—our mind; because as we think, so we are.

Each day, we are bombarded with thoughts that can affect moods and human behavior and we have to know how to deal with our thought life. Philippians 4:8–9 gives us a whole checklist of things we should daily inventory in our thought life.

- "Finally, brethren, whatsoever things are true, whatsoever things are honest, whatsoever things are just, whatsoever things are pure, whatsoever things are lovely, whatsoever things are of good report; if there be any virtue, and if there be any praise, think on these things. Those things, which ye have both learned, and received, and heard, and seen in me, do: and the God of peace shall be with you"—Philippians 4:8–9.

If we cast our burdens on the Lord, no matter what they are, we can have a winner's mentality each day of our lives.

The Bible says:

- "And be not conformed to this world, but be ye transformed by the renewing of your mind . . ."—Romans 12:2.

This is a powerful tool in knowing how to transform from defeat to victory, from the negative to the positive, and from ordinary to extraordinary.

God didn't create any of us to be taken down by the storms of life. But He created us to be "more than conquerors" through Christ Jesus our Lord! (Romans 8:37.)

And then, there's the all important self-talk:

Self-talk is simply encouraging your own self with the many positive affirmations from the Word of God.

Never allow negative words to be spoken over you or people who are significant in your life!

Words are thoughts expressed. When we began to express the Word of God our lives are changed, even if it seems to be imperceptible change at first.

The *New Living Translation* of Ephesians 4:25 says:

- "Let everything you say be good and helpful, so that your words will be an encouragement to those who hear them."

Self-talk allows us to change our focus even when our circumstances haven't changed!

David had such a heart after God. He faced a storm at a place called Ziklag. (But please remember, we have to have our "Ziklag" before our Zion.)

David and his men had been away from the city for a few days and when they returned they could not believe the devastation that was before them. The whole city had been burned with fire and the children taken away and the women ravaged.

David literally wept until there was no more power to weep. But he used the key I have used in so many of life's storms. David began to encourage himself in the Lord!

Read about this story in I Samuel 30. This is one of the greatest chapters on the power of self-talk that you ever find in the Bible. This is how David overcame one of the greatest tragedies of his life.

Wright

Jana, there are people who have faced agonizing reversals in their lives. Is there a way for a person who has faced total collapse and failure to get back up and recover from the "tsunamis" of life?

Jana

First of all, nobody has to remain a victim. There are basic reasons why people fail. Whatever your failure may be, and whatever the reason, God wants it to be a signal that it's time for change. Pain is simply an indicator. God has a message for you. And God speaks through the traumatic places of life.

A tsunami leaves a trail of devastation. I don't know what has happened in your life to leave you in the middle of nothing but ashes, but I know that God is greater than the past and He specializes in the very things that men call impossible. And whenever you come into obedience to Him, He longs to bless you and make your life bigger, better, and stronger than you thought it could possibly be.

God's takes weak things to confound the wise:

- But God hath chosen the foolish things of the world to confound the wise; and God hath chosen the weak things of the world to confound the things which are mighty."—I Corinthians 1:27

We would never pick a David or a Peter for our team or even a Jana Alcorn, but God takes delight in taking despised vessels and making them into vessels of honor. Your situation is perfect for God.

We have to let go of the old. I have an old car in my garage and I have a new car. Each day I have to decide if I am going to drive the old car or the new one. It is a choice that I make. I can't drive them both at the same time. I have to choose. In other words, we have to let go of the past.

God told the Israelites that the Egyptians they saw today, they would see again no more forever:

- "And Moses said unto the people, Fear ye not, stand still, and see the salvation of the Lord, which he will show to you to day: for the Egyptians whom ye have seen to day, ye shall see them again no more for ever."—Exodus 14:13

Similarly, we leave the failures of the past to never live there again. The windshield is so much larger than the rear view mirror.

Failure is an open door to the future. It is not your prison, so walk out. Jesus Christ was anointed by the Holy Spirit for the purpose of delivering the captive. Your prison doors are open; why are you staying in? The prison of fear, defeat, discouragements, and so many other captive places have been dealt with in the finished work of Christ. When Jesus said, "It is finished," He meant that the great plan of redemption was finally accomplished. Consequently, you are free! So go free!

God says:

- "Behold, I will do a new thing . . ."—Isaiah 43:19

Now, let me ask you a question: Which do you want, old or new? It is up to you.

Failure is not final. And remember, as Zig Ziglar says, "Failure is an event, not a person."

Moses' storm was a personal failure. He was a fugitive on the run when God called Him. But not only did God bring him out of Midian, he went on to lead the greatest move in the history of God's chosen people.

David experienced personal failure even after killing Goliath and being a household word in Israel. Everybody in the land knew of his failure, but God chose to refine and purify David in his own way. He became the greatest King in Israel, left us with the wonderful book of Psalms, was an intimate worshipper of his King, and Jesus Himself was called the "Son of David."

I'm sure those with a "religious" mindset would have marked David off their list, but God is the God of infinite mercy and His mercies are new every morning:

- "It is of the Lord's mercies that we are not consumed, because his compassions fail not. They are new every morning: great is thy faithfulness."—Lamentations 3:22–23

There is no condemnation to those who are in Christ Jesus:

- "There is therefore now no condemnation to them which are in Christ Jesus, who walk not after the flesh, but after the spirit . . ."—Romans 8:1

Begin to value what God values and understand that God values you!

- "He has chosen us in Him before the foundation of the world . . ."—Ephesians 1:4

You don't have to earn the love of God and you can never lose it! Build value in yourself. We are told to love our neighbors as ourselves (Matt. 22:39, Mark 12:31, Luke 10:27, etc.). We can't love our neighbor until we first learn to love ourselves. Don't let others determine your value now. Get back to what the Lord values and build self-worth in order to maximize His plan through your life!

The enemy fears your future. That's why there is such a battle. That's why you feel that failure is final. But God has a greater yes.

Perhaps you have faced the storm of a personal failure. Be cleansed by the blood of Jesus in your life and get up and move on in God! The best is yet to come. God is a Master Restorer and He knows just how to make you a trophy of His grace. There's more in you than you know. God has not changed His mind about you. Your circumstances have not contradicted the promises of God in your life—they are merely a prerequisite for all that God has for you! God's day begins in the evening and I can promise you, the sun will shine again!

Wright

Storms can be so stripping and so depleting. Jana, how do people make it who have no support systems in place?

Alcorn

Isolation is a storm in itself. When captors want to torture their prisoners, they are put into isolation. Isolation is cruel and torturous. We were made to connect. However, there may be times in life when you must be prepared for isolation. The reasons could be varied, but the pain is still overwhelming. As in any challenge, however, there can be positive things derived. I think it is important to reap the benefits of isolation and not to merely focus on the pain of isolation.

David, called and anointed, found himself tending sheep when he knew that kingship was his destiny! The lonely life he led was a requirement placed upon him by God Himself, for it was David who would teach us the spiritual benefits of meditating upon the Lord. How did David learn this truth and come to share so many sweet psalms with the world? He did it through overcoming the storm of isolation. Oh, what a storm this can be!

The storm of isolation can be agonizing; but remember that you are never alone and there is always One praying for you and with you:

- "Wherefore he is able also to save them to the uttermost that come unto God by him, seeing he ever liveth to make intercession for them."—Hebrews 7:25
- "For he hath said, I will never leave thee, nor forsake thee."—Hebrews 13:5

- "God is our refuge and strength, a very present help in trouble."—Psalm 46:1

Even if you have absolutely *no* support system, if you are a believer in Jesus Christ and have accepted Him as your personal Lord and Savior, then everything you need He has already placed within you. Your future is not in someone else—your future is inside of you. When the King lives on the inside, believe me, He will go hang His own flag on the porch!

Become an army of one and move forward with your life!

Wright
There are people who have been rejected, betrayed, and abandoned. Jana, what has the Holy Spirit shown you that will help others overcome these kinds of storms?

Alcorn
Rejection, abandonment, controversy, and criticism can send a person to an emotional grave quickly. Psychologists tell us that to be abandoned by a person who should receive us is one of the most psychologically devastating events of life.

Joseph thought his brothers would be overjoyed by his dreams, but instead it was these same brothers who stripped him, beat him, left him in a dry hole and finally sold him as a slave. You can read the entire story in Genesis 37:23–28.

The storms of abandonment damage the soul of mankind. Are you in a storm of abandonment? I can imagine that Joseph's own mind became his worst enemy in this storm. Surely he would die in a foreign land and never fulfill the dream God had given him. How mentally torturous are the storms of abandonment and rejection!

The Apostle Paul told us that he was abandoned at the worst possible time:

- "We are troubled on every side, yet not distressed; we are perplexed, but not in despair; Persecuted, but not forsaken; cast down, but not destroyed; Always bearing about in the body the dying of the Lord Jesus, that the life also of Jesus might be made manifest in our body."—2 Corinthians 4:8–10

Have you ever been abandoned at just the moment that you needed a helping hand the very most in life? Have you ever reached out with an urgency that resembled panic, only to discover that the ones you knew would never leave you are now gone? The storms of abandonment and rejection are some of the most brutal of life. Endure the pressure and press on anyway!

What a relief to know that you can run and hide in the face of Jesus Christ!

- "For in the time of trouble he shall hide me in his pavilion: in the secret of his tabernacle shall he hide me; he shall set me up upon a rock."—Psalm 27:5

We must never forget our Lord Jesus in the Garden of Gethsemane. If He had ever needed His disciples to "stay in the foxhole" with Him, it was at this crucial point, however, just at the moment of His most intense preparation in prayer, He was abandoned. They failed to stand with Him even after He had given instructions to watch:

- "And saith unto them, My soul is exceeding sorrowful unto death: tarry ye here, and watch. And he went forward a little, and fell on the ground, and prayed that, if it were possible, the hour might pass from him. And he said, Abba, Father, all things are possible unto thee; take away this cup from me: nevertheless not what I will, but what thou wilt. And he cometh, and findeth them sleeping, and saith unto Peter, Simon, sleepest thou? couldest not thou watch one hour? Watch ye and pray, lest ye enter into temptation. The spirit truly is ready, but the flesh is weak. And again he went away, and prayed, and spake the same words. And when he returned, he found them asleep again, (for their eyes were heavy,) neither wist they what to answer him. And he cometh the third time, and saith unto them, Sleep on now, and take your rest: it is enough, the hour is come; behold, the Son of man is betrayed into the hands of sinners."—Mark 14:34–41

Remember, at whatever station of life you find yourself, Jesus has already been there. He saw everything, he heard everything, and He is there. Settle it in your heart that Jesus will never, and I mean *never*, leave you. Wherever He is taking you, you can get there from here! And He has promised to be with you!

Wright

You know, Jana, any of these storms could have a tendency to stack themselves on top of one another. What do you say to someone facing a financial challenge, even while in the middle of these other things?

Alcorn

Financial storms can come without any fault of our own. Often we are misjudged when the financial storm comes. But the cause of the storm is not the most important thing to the Lord because the storms beat upon the just and the unjust. God just wants to put you in touch with your Foundation so that you will know that you know that you know that whatever the weapon formed against you, it will not prosper

- "No weapon that is formed against thee shall prosper; and every tongue that shall rise against thee in judgment thou shalt condemn. This is the heritage of the servants of the Lord, and their righteousness is of me, saith the Lord."— Isaiah 54:17

Your reaction to the storm is what will make the difference.

The Bible gives an excellent story about a woman who faced several challenges all at once. The widow woman in II Kings 4 was "a certain woman of the wives of the sons of the prophets."

After her husband's passing, she not only faced the storm of the death of a loved one, but now she was going to lose her only two sons to debtor's prison for seven years! But I thought the Scriptures said to:

- "Believe His prophets and so shall you prosper!"—2 Chron. 20:20

Why wasn't that working for her? After all, she was married to a son of a prophet! So this is a good Old Testament example of someone who faced multiple storms at the same time. Her storms involved the spiritual, relational, emotional, social, and even financial.

The storm of financial adversity knocked on her door, and it was going to try to take away all she had left. God had a blessing in disguise. He was going to use it to provide a lifetime income for her and her sons. God has the power to make this financial storm—and any storm—a blessing!

It is important at the moment of financial crisis that you keep God first in your finances.

Let me share some principles to help you overcome during a time of financial adversity:

- Firstly, always remember that God specializes in the impossible. Your situation may be impossible for you, but it certainly is not impossible for God. Don't give up on the God factor!
- Secondly, harness the power of prayer. Jeremiah says to call on God:
- Call unto me, and I will answer thee, and show thee great and mighty things, which thou knowest not."—Jeremiah 33:3
- Jesus taught us to pray for provision in His model prayer as recorded in Matthew 6. Go boldly to the throne of grace.
- Then, rehearse the laws of sowing and reaping. Have you been faithful to sow financial seeds into good soil? If you have sown bountifully, you can reap bountifully. If you have not been obedient to the Holy Spirit in this area, then just go to the Lord and repent and turn, and believe God for a supernatural reversal!
- Make sure your house is in order. Have you repented of all known sin? Have you repented from actions and thoughts, unforgiveness, bitterness? Have you released those who have wronged you? Do you have the right motive? Do you desire to be a blessing to the Kingdom of God and to others? God says we have to take care of these things. First the natural, then the spiritual as the Bible indicates in I Corinthians 15. Then take care of hidden sins that weight you down:
  "Wherefore seeing we also are compassed about with so great a cloud of witnesses, let us lay aside every weight, and the sin which doth so easily beset us, and

let us run with patience the race that is set before us."—Hebrews 12:1

- And then, review your resources. This could be a time for something as simple as a yard sale or as complex as a corporate rearrangement. Reviewing may led to revising. Be flexible.

Please know that God delights in the prosperity of His servants:

"Let them shout for joy, and be glad, that favor my righteous cause: yea, let them say continually, Let the Lord be magnified, which hath pleasure in the prosperity of his servant."—Psalm 35:27

Establish some goals, get a plan, maintain your confession as you continue to plant your seeds, and then let faith and patience have its perfect work!

Wright

Wow Jana! I believe that so many are on the verge of tremendous breakthroughs. I know you have gleaned these principles from the furnace of trials in your own life. The Bible says that iron sharpens iron:

- "Iron sharpeneth iron; so a man sharpeneth the countenance of his friend."—Proverbs 27:17

So we know that you have undoubtedly encountered challenges in relationships. Tell us about overcoming in the area of relationships.

Alcorn

David, relationships are the most important thing in the world. God has made all of us for connection. He has made us for relationships that will bless our lives and be mutually enriching. But in this, life can be full of questions. You and I don't have all the answers. If you have ever asked God questions about your relationships, then I believe that God is ready to give some answers.

Sometimes we are attacked relationally for different reasons. Satan wants to rob us of every one of our healthy relationships.

- "Two are better than one, because they have a good reward for their labor. For if they fall down, the one will lift
  up his fellow: but woe to him that is alone when he fal-
  leth; for he hath not another to help him up."—
  Ecclesiastes 4:9–10

God sets the solitary in families so that chains can be broken.

- Psalm 68:6: "God setteth the solitary in families: he
  bringeth out those which are bound with chains: but the
  rebellious dwell in a dry land."

One person can be our key to various forms of bondage being broken. The onslaught against relationships weakens the delivering
power of God. Satan will do anything to break the power of unity in
our relationships. Strife in marriage hinders the working of the Holy
Spirit.

- "Likewise, ye husbands, dwell with them according to
  knowledge, giving honor unto the wife, as unto the
  weaker vessel, and as being heirs together of the grace of
  life; that your prayers be not hindered."—I Peter 3:7

The Apostle Paul counted on his relationship with Timothy. Paul
was imprisoned and he counted on Timothy for comfort. He asked for
Timothy to come to him before the cold of winter set in.

- "The cloak that I left at Troas with Carpus, when thou
  comest, bring with thee, and the books, but especially the
  parchments."—2 Timothy 4:13

But even in prison, he recognized that his books and his "Bible"
were his friends. He asked for the books, and especially the parchments. In times of relational challenge, our Bible and our books can
become our friends.

But there is nothing like Christianity clothed in humanity. Paul
chose Mark to accompany him on his missionary tours. When Jesus
came, He came to relate to us. He identified with us. That's why the
Bible records in John 1:14:

- "The Word became flesh . . . "

- "Again I say unto you, that if two of you shall agree on earth as touching anything that they shall ask, it shall be done for them . . . "—Matthew 18:19.

This is powerful.

Even Jesus prayed for our unity and union in the Body of Christ:

- "That they all may be one."—John 17:21

There are two kinds of people in our lives: People who add and people who subtract.

When I think of relationships, I think of the example of our Lord Jesus. He had people who leaned on Him, a handpicked friend who betrayed him, Peter, the disciple who denied Him, the ever-loving Mary, and the busy Martha. He had brothers and he had a mother who refused to desert her son when he was in distress. He had an earthly adoptive father who taught him skill and business. He had business relationships and a traveling team. He went through the gamut of relationships as our Supreme Example. He taught us conflict management and connection. He gave us principles in the Word that will enable us to stop the assignment of the enemy against our relationships.

If we have offended someone, we can go to him or her. The person may not receive us, but we can still go. And we can learn to practice what my husband used to call "instant forgiveness" (I like that); because Christ forgave us, we can forgive others.

I have been so blessed to know the meaning of the most important relationship on this earth and that is within my own marriage. Bill and I had so many mountains to shout about in our marriage and we had a lot of valleys to walk through, but the basis of all of it was love.

Wright

Jana, so many people are fighting the good fight of faith right now. Crisis has changed your life. Tell us about your experience in walking through the valley of the shadow of death.

Alcorn

David, I'd like to close our interview by talking about the storm of death. Maybe it is a physical death or the death of a dream or the end of something meaningful in your life.

When someone or something has died we can only trust God for His perspective. Remember, there can be no resurrection without a death.

When Bill and I received word from the doctors that he only had months to live, we were crushed and heartbroken and spent the first few days hugging and crying and praying minute by minute for the Lord's grace. Once we made the decision to quickly tell our son, we began to pray for the Lord's strength to let our little son know that Daddy was very, very sick, but that our total hope and trust was in God's unfailing faithfulness. We also needed to let Jordan know that the medicine for Dad could possibly make it even seem to be worse.

Our home has always been a refuge and a happy place to be. In fact, it still is our favorite place on earth. As Bill and I walked through the chemo-battle, the one-hour drive each way back and forth from our house to the hospital became our place of undistracted heart-to-heart talks. It was on one of these drives that I had to tell Bill that after all the poisonous intravenous chemo drugs, after all the sickness as a result of the treatments, the hospital stays, and the emotional torture of this kind of diagnosis, the cancerous tumors were still growing. I had learned the results of the CT scan days before, but didn't feel the timing was right for me to tell him. I had watched his weight freefall and we had labored together in prayer for his healing to manifest. The battle had been so hard. And this whole process was moving so very fast.

It was on this drive, as I was driving as slowly as I could, that Bill began to open his heart to me with such tenderness. He said to me, "Honey, I want our relationship to be so real that we can always tell each other everything and never hold anything back." As he was talking, I was thinking that he already knew everything about me and that I already knew everything about him. After almost twenty years of marriage, you learn almost everything. And we both were talkers and enjoyed endless conversations on almost every topic of life.

This is when the Holy Spirit spoke to my heart and gently said, "Now is the time to tell him about the CT scan."

I said to him, "Bill," as I glanced over to his side of the car, "would you want us to tell each other *everything* even if it hurt so bad and you knew it would hurt the other one?"

And he looked penetratingly at me with the most firm, yet gentle and loving look and tone and said simply, "Yes."

I immediately knew what I had to do and do it right then. We would only have less than one precious hour before we would be seeing the oncologist who would give him this grim report in the coldness of an oncology office.

I looked at him and said quickly. "I know the results of the CT scan."

He said, "You do?"

I said, "Yes, they're growing." Then our hearts just began to bleed together, once again.

With that, we began our decision to forego the final chemo treatment. When we arrived at the hospital, the oncologists told us that, in spite of aggressive treatment and the most cutting edge drugs available, that this cancerous invasion had only multiplied and grew. He stated to us that he saw no need in any further treatments or appointments. We agreed and left.

We realized then that we had come to the end of every natural plan. Now was the real test, not just of our faith, but also of our trust in our eternal Lord and Savior. This would be when our faith would graduate to trust.

Looking back, God had given me slight preparations. In January of 2005, I was standing in the Waves of Light Radio Studio in Managua, Nicaragua. There were about four hundred Nicaraguans in the studio that day; our global team was doing a "live" broadcast, reaching one hundred thousand souls throughout Central America. I was in the middle of a very deep traumatic, emotional storm. Standing there that morning with my hands raised in worship, the tears began to stream down my cheeks. I had told the Lord that I didn't even know if I had the strength to go out and minister to the children who lived at the garbage dump as we had planned.

Just at that moment, with the pain in my heart unbearable, the Lord spoke to me and said two simple words. It was the way that He spoke them—the calmness—the gentleness, yet the firmness. The velvet and the steel: "Trust Me." I could not have had an idea of the storm that was yet to come!

When God tells you to trust Him, brace yourself. There is going to be opportunity for obedience. Through the storms, no matter what you name them, continue to trust. Trust Him when you can't trace Him! That night before I went to sleep, the Holy Spirit impressed me to read the Psalm from the date of the day, which happened to be the eleventh day of the month.

I read through tear-filled eyes:

- "In the Lord put I my trust: how say ye to my soul, Flee as a bird to your mountain?"—Psalm 11:1

I only needed a few words, "In thee O Lord do I put my trust." I closed my Bible. He had spoken.

Seven months later, on August 11, 2005, my precious life's partner and best friend, with my arms around him, went home to be with the Lord. That evening our son and I, along with my mother, said good-bye to our friends and church family who had come to comfort us. I then sat down alone in Bill's favorite chair. I wept and touched the arms of the chair where he had sat only hours before. I said to the Lord, "Lord, my heart is completely shattered. I am totally broken." Our little son, who had just turned twelve, was in so much agony. "Lord, I just need something from your Word."

I felt the Holy Spirit speak lovingly to my heart, "Turn to the Psalm of the day." Once again it happened to be the eleventh day of the month. I turned without thinking of my experience earlier in Nicaragua. As I looked at Psalm 11:1, I saw a note scribbled on the side: "Nicaragua 1-11-05." I sobbed with a broken heart as I again read through eyes that were so swollen, tired, and grieving, "In Thee O Lord, do I put my trust." I closed my Bible. He had spoken.

As my head fell upon the arms of the chair, with Bill's identifying smell still lingering, I knew that I had instructions for me and for our son. Trust. Trust Him. Trust Him when you can't trace Him. When you've lost everything, trust Him. When you don't understand, trust Him. When you have to say goodbye to someone you love, trust Him. When you're a young widow and have a little son to raise without a dad, trust Him. When you don't know what tomorrow holds, but you know Who holds tomorrow, trust Him.

God has an appointment with each of us in the place called total trust. Just like God spoke to Jeremiah to go to the Potter's House and He was going to reveal something to Him:

- "Arise, and go down to the potter's house, and there I will cause thee to hear my words."—Jeremiah 18:2

There is a fire for each one of us; we just don't know what it will be.

Every builder knows that the higher the building, the deeper into the ground you have to go. God allows us to be drilled deeply because He has great plans for us. And He loves us enough to process us through the storms of life so that when we come through it, our lives are more enriched and we become more like the Lord!

No matter what kind of storm you are in, never give up. Keep your eyes on the Lord and trust Him through all of life's stormy winds! God has the power to raise both you and your dreams from this very place! No matter what.

- "And we know that all things work together for good to them that love God, to them who are the called according to His purpose."—Romans 8:28

About the Author

JANA ALCORN is an author, conference speaker, and motivational coach. Impacting over forty nations of the world, she equips for Kingdom advancement. She is the founder of Dream Child Foundation and Hayley's House, an African orphanage. She is also Founder of Dream Builders Network, utilizing apostolic strategies including leadership development. She received her educational training at Southwestern College and the University of Alabama. She received her Bachelor of Theology from Christian Bible College. She shares in mutual accountability and integrity through Vertical Apostolic Covering. She is a widow and mother of one son, Jordan L. Alcorn. They make their home in North Alabama.

Jana Alcorn

Jana Alcorn Ministries

P.O. Box 4500

Huntsville, Alabama 35815

Phone: 256.470.0454

E-mail: Info@JanaAlcorn.com

Web site: www.JanaAlcorn.com

Chapter 6

LONNA VOPAT

David E. Wright (Wright)

Today we're talking with Lonna Vopat who is a nationally known ministry speaker and television talk show host. As a participant in the 2002 Mrs. America Beauty Pageant, the Lord opened the door for Lonna to share her faith from many platforms across the country and internationally. Her passion is to inspire people to find their hope and healing in Jesus Christ. The Lord has blessed Lonna with the gift to communicate His word with boldness, compassion, and humor. Lonna, her husband Kevin, and their three children enjoy their country home in Idaho. For more information about her and her ministry you can go to the Web site www.in-his-grace.com.

Lonna, welcome to *Speaking of Faith*.

Vopat

Thank you David, I am delighted to be a part of the *Speaking of Faith* project.

Wright

So tell us, how did you begin in the speaking ministry?

Vopat

My speaking ministry began in a very unusual and unconventional way. It began as a result of my participation in the nationally televised 2002 Mrs. America pageant. I had become involved with the pageant at the state level—Mrs. Idaho, America—through a series of events.

The first event was a phone call from the state director asking me to consider participating in the pageant. My initial reaction was to hang up the phone and run away fast! But through a lot of prayer and seeing doors opening, I began to realize what an opportunity this could be. I was encouraged by friends to use the pageant as a platform to share information about an inner city ministry I'd worked with for several years called Cup of Cool Water (CCW) in Spokane, Washington. CCW is an outreach to homeless and street youth, ages ten to twenty-two; I have a real passion for these lost kids. I turned that passion into an opportunity to share the desperate plight of these youth with people across our state. I never thought I would walk away from that event with the crown and title because my pageant performance during the competition was so pitiful. It resembled an episode of "I Love Lucy," from tripping on stage to stepping on and tearing out the hem of my evening gown during competition! However, the outcome of the pageant confirmed to me that God has very creative ways of using His children.

I was extremely verbal about my faith during that event, I felt as though the Lord had called me there to pray and encourage the other contestants. Just three months later at the Mrs. America pageant I found my purpose once again was to pray, encourage, and witness for the Lord.

It was shortly after my Mrs. America experience that I started receiving calls to speak and share my faith. During my devotion and prayer time the Lord began putting together my signature presentation, "From Maybelline to the Maker." This presentation focuses on the world's obsession with beauty and the astounding lengths women will go in striving to achieve it. I had a front row seat at Mrs. America to observe this and it broke my heart. "Maybelline" shares my pageant experiences in humorous ways, because let's face it; there are some pretty comical aspects to beauty pageants.

I also use props and my personal testimony to share the message of true beauty, not the fallacy the media has saturated society with, but God's definition of beauty. I did the first "Maybelline" presentation for fifty women in the meeting room of a restaurant in my hometown. It was very rough and unpolished but the response was amazing. I knew then the Lord had designed it to encourage women in this very real struggle they have with body image and self-esteem in today's world.

Wright

So where did the name "In His Grace" come from?

Vopat

Because of the number of speaking requests coming in, my husband and I felt strongly that the Lord was turning my speaking opportunities into a full time ministry. As I began to pray earnestly about this ministry and what it would be called the Lord brought to mind "in His grace." It immediately touched my heart because that is how I live life daily—*in His grace.*

Wright

You know, most conferences now have a lot of advice for women about how to balance their career and family life. I imagine that, like everyone, you know the importance of it; but you live it day in and day out, don't you? How do you balance career and family life?

Vopat

I have many women ask me that, because between the speaking ministry, the talk show, and book projects it seems impossible to fit everything in *and* be a wife and mom. This is how I see it: my first and most important ministry is my role in our home. The Lord gave me the honor of being a wife to my husband, Kevin. He also gave me the absolute privilege of being Mom to Parker, Dillon, and Grace. I don't take that responsibility lightly. One thing we recognize in our family is we don't differentiate between "Mom on stage" and "Mom at home." The only difference is the location. My husband and I have raised our kids with the understanding that as believers—as Christians—our mission field is every place we are. We have a responsibility to reach out to the people we come in contact with, sharing our faith through our words and our actions. For our children it is at school, in church youth group, or extracurricular activities. For my husband it is at his job, and in the community. For me it's wherever the Lord places me, whether it is in front of an audience or in the grocery store buying milk. Just because I'm in front of an audience talking about Jesus doesn't mean that when the lights are off my ministry is over. Truthfully that is when my ministry begins. We know there is no separation between a public ministry and our private lives, because our life *is* our ministry.

As far as balancing the aspect of having three kids and being on the road, I could not do it without our folks. I have great family support. Our folks are retired and live quite close to us. They are able to help out with the kids when I am traveling. My husband is the backbone of this ministry. I run all my speaking engagements by him and we are in agreement about where I am going to go. Invitations come in that could fill up my whole year. My family is so important that we limit my speaking invitations through prayer and listening to the Lord's guidance.

Wright

It's interesting to me that you've said your ministry really begins immediately after your presentations. Would you tell us a little bit about that?

Vopat

When I share "From Maybelline to the Maker" or a different message, I believe the Lord shares with the audience what it is He wants them to hear through His Word on that occasion. When I come off the platform I always make sure, in every venue, that I have an opportunity to visit with the audience. This is truly when the ministry starts, it's when the fellowship happens, and it is exciting. When women can share their pain, heartbreaks, and victories with me it is wonderful. Most people can relate to my personal testimony at some level and it really gives me a chance to encourage them in the Word and to pray with them.

I receive e-mails and letters after events updating me on transformations that have taken place in the lives of these women. The bondages that the Lord can break and the victory that He claims over lives is awesome to see. Glory be to God!

Wright

You know, I enjoy asking people how they define success because I get almost a different answer each time, so I'm going to ask you the same question. What do you consider success to be?

Vopat

I have to admit that I struggle with society's definition of success. We are living in a time and generation of "it's all about me." Success is gauged in such different ways. Many people believe a successful person is the one who has the most celebrity and money. I couldn't disagree more. All you have to do is ask someone who has all those things if they have peace, happiness, and are content in life and you will probably get a resounding "No!" These things do not bring you happiness!

Success to me is defined by being in the center of God's will—wherever God places me whether it's within a ministry in my church Sunday school, flipping burgers, or on a stage in front of 5,000 people. Success is not the number of people who admire you, or the amount of money you make, but in doing God's will in your life. I guarantee you there is no more peaceful and satisfying place than right there. Those worldly things will pass away but God's design and purpose for my life is what really excites and encourages me.

Another aspect of success lies within our family life. As a wife, success is seeing that God is in the center of my marriage. As a mother, success is seeing that my kids love the Lord and desire to serve Him with their lives. That is my definition of success—it totally goes against the world's concept and idea of success.

Wright

I was going to ask you what you think the biggest obstacles are that people face in trying to become successful but let me see if I can consider this a little bit, based on what you just said. If I were trying to become successful, in your definition, *not* trying to ascertain what the will of God would be for my life would really be an obstacle wouldn't it?

Vopat

Absolutely! I find that the first mistake people make in reaching for success is they want it to be about them. They want it to be about what they can *get* in this world, not about what they can *give*. When will we learn it is not about the *getting* that makes life purposeful but it's about *giving* that brings joy to your life? Here we go again—it is that "all about me attitude." You know, the problem with this mentality is the enemy will use it as a stumbling block every time. When you are focused on "self" you have let the enemy get a foothold in your life. When you have your focus on God it seems like your path becomes smoother, the obstacles you're facing are more easily removed and there is victory. It does not mean you don't go through pain and hardships but it means you go through those trials with the strength, the knowledge, the confidence, and the peace that only comes from the Lord.

I do believe that the Lord blesses people financially or with recognition. But those blessings come with responsibility, accountability, and the necessity to keep it in perspective and most importantly that they glorify God with them. It is a matter of acknowledging that every blessing comes from God. Let's face it, it all belongs to God anyway. When people get fixated on obtaining wealth, worldly success, and attention it becomes the biggest stumbling block there is. We can say, "It's all about me," but God is the Creator and He knows better. We were created to give glory to God not to live for ourselves.

Wright

It is interesting—to non-believers it *is* all about them and that's a shame. What would you say to someone whose life experiences have left them empty and doubting they have anything to offer?

Vopat

What we have to realize is when we are empty, hopeless, and in the bottom of the pit, that is when we have a tremendous amount to offer. When we are broken and hurting and there's barely enough energy to get up in the morning, that is when we can truly abandon ourselves to the Lord's strength.

I've been there, I have been at the bottom of the pit. I understand what it feels like to be completely hopeless. After two failed suicide attempts, I know what it feels like to believe there is nothing to live for. It is when we are there that Jesus is able to take our hand and pull us out of the mire. We are so useable when we are completely vulnerable and have nothing left to fight against God with.

When you get down to it, whether it is in ministry, business, or our families, all we have to offer is ourselves. I know the impact of that statement because when I share my testimony I see the effect it has on the people I am speaking to. When they hear how desperate I was and what a wretch I was before coming to Christ, that is when they can see that ray of light—that ray of hope—which comes from having Christ as your Savior. God made each of us divinely in His image; He has a tremendous purpose for each life He created. Even though our nature is to doubt that, it is all in the Scriptures. The most important question you have to ask yourself when you are in that place is, "Do you believe God?"

Wright

So how would you encourage someone to let go of past failures or accomplishments, hurts, pains, and memories?

Vopat

The encouragement I can give is to simply allow the Lord to use your past with all its pain to show how big Jesus Christ's grace and mercy are. It really takes determination and a strong will to let go of failure. I know I used my past as body armor; I would wear it because it was my defense to keep me from being hurt, blocking out the world. What God showed me was that armor was broken, weak, and insufficient. He showed me how to put on the armor of Christ, which is strong and impenetrable. It is what is going to protect me in this world. My own pride and holding on to my past failures is not going to protect me from anything. What that will do is cloak me in shame, regret, and painful memories. That is not what God's design is for us. He wants to lift us out of that place to live a life of joy, and triumph over our past.

Wright

You know, it occurs to me that a suicide attempt is real serious. In the face of all you have experienced how do you view your circumstances now in comparison with how you viewed them at that time?

Vopat

Oh, completely different. I had to break away from my victim mentality. Sometimes when we've had bad things happen in life we allow ourselves to be identified as victims. We tend to use a victim mentality in every aspect of our lives. For years I lived with an attitude of "woe is me." I would take this attitude into relationships or work and express it to my family and friends. This became extremely destructive in my life, in fact it sabotaged some potentially wonderful blessings.

I prefer to say that I am a survivor and the only reason I survived is because I climbed into the lifeboat of Christ. As a survivor of physical and sexual abuse in my childhood I allowed that label to keep me in chains. I believed I was unloved and unworthy and, let me tell you David, it put me in a rapid downward spiral. For years I didn't tell anyone about the abuse I experienced; I lived in shame and agony. It was truly a living hell. But when Jesus released me from that ugliness, He showed me my identity was certainly not as a victim, but as a *victor*. He showed me through His Word, abundant love, and grace that I was His child. I was made in His image and I was wonderful in His sight.

To know the Creator of the universe loves me beyond measure is the identity I want to live in, not as a victim. Victory happens when we grasp God's Truth that we are able to shed that unproductive and harmful victim mentality. Then we are able to live our life with peace and confidence. Each one of us has that promise with Christ.

Wright

So what's been the toughest thing you've ever gone through?

Vopat

That is not an easy question. Probably the hardest thing I've experienced was my mother's death in 1992. It brought up a myriad of emotions I was not ready to deal with. My parents divorced when I was four years old and my dad took on the responsibility of raising my older brother and me as a single parent.

At that time my mom could not take on the responsibility of two young children. Due to these circumstances our relationship was very unhealthy. She was unable to grasp the responsibility of being a mother; but through the years we muddled through it.

Two years before her untimely death in 1992, she came into a beautiful relationship with Jesus Christ. Our relationship was healed and restored when she accepted Christ as her Savior. We had a glorious two years together, which included the birth of my first son, Parker. She was able to experience the joy of being a grandmother. It was such a healing time. Her death was sudden and unexpected and when it happened it sent me into a tailspin. I thought, "Finally I have the mother I had always hoped and dreamed of and then the Lord took her." I have to admit I was pretty angry with God for several years; but He was gentle, loving, and tender with me. We worked through it together and a lot of healing took place in my heart. Spiritually my relationship with Him was strengthened and renewed during that time.

Today my feelings have completely changed about my mother's death. I have peace knowing that one day I'll be with her. I know she is living with Jesus and it will be a wonderful reunion.

Wright

When in your life have you felt God's presence in a strong, undeniable way?

Vopat

There have been many times when I have been reading the Word and a scripture has just leaped out at me. It was exactly what I needed to hear and the direction I needed to be given. If you have experienced those "God moments," you know what I mean. God is so faithful. It is as if the Lord is speaking directly into my ear—it's just amazing.

There are other times when the Lord has made himself known when I am disobedient. I get a spiritual spanking and it hurts. But I've come to a place in my relationship with Him where I appreciate these moments in my spiritual life because they are a reminder of how much He loves me and how much He desires to shape me into His likeness. It is still painful, don't get me wrong, but I desire that reprimanding because I really want to live my life for Him.

Another experience is before I go out and speak or before I start my day, often I am brought to tears during my prayer time because His presence is so strong around me, especially when I am sharing His Word. I'm not foolish enough to think that I'm a great speaker, David; anything I share comes from the Lord. I am simply a girl with a story and a deep love for Jesus. I know that my own strength and my own knowledge is not enough to equip me to do what I do in this ministry. It is only through the Lord and His abundance that I'm able to share His Word and the salvation message. Not in my power but in His.

Wright

In your life experiences, when did you know He was walking with you? How did you know for sure?

Vopat

I will share one example that stands out in my life. This happened when I was twenty years old and I share this in my testimony. I was on the verge of a second suicide attempt because I had hit rock bottom. I felt there was nothing left to live for—nothing. I knew the Lord—I had asked him to be my Savior when I was thirteen at Bible camp. However due to the pain of my childhood I used drugs, alcohol, and promiscuous behavior to numb the pain. I had strayed away from Him. All this had led me down a really horrible road and by the time I was twenty, I hate to say it, I had been in painful and extremely abusive relationships. I had made some very dangerous choices in my life. One of those was the decision to have an abortion. I had made that choice twice by the time I was twenty. I had just really damaged myself beyond what I believed could be healed and repaired. I was the epitome of brokenness.

One night, after I had been drinking and was alone in my apartment, I decided that I was done. I felt useless, worthless, and I knew my life had hit rock bottom. I retrieved a gun from my bedroom closet that a friend had given me for protection. I remember loading it and being in a heap on the floor sobbing. It was at that moment when I felt God's hand on my shoulder. I knew it was His hand and I put the gun down on the floor. I grabbed that hand and David, it was tangible—it was the hand of God and it was gripping mine. I cried out and said, "Lord, if you can forgive me, if you can use this pitiful person lying on the floor before you, if you can take me out of this hell, I will serve you with my life."

In that moment He literally scooped me up off the floor and into His arms. As He held me He said, "I have been waiting for you. Welcome home daughter." Jesus made Himself known in such a tangible, emotional way that I knew He was not just a vapor, He was not just a pretty sunset, He was not something the pastor spoke about from the pulpit—He was real and He wanted to be the Lord of my life.

Wright

Interesting. Are you up for one more question?

Vopat

Of course!

Wright

Would you name some of the things in life you really treasure the most?

Vopat

Chocolate, sleeping past seven in the morning, a clean house . . . (I'm just kidding.) All these things are wonderful but not at the top of my list. I think this question is the easiest one you have asked me. All joking aside, the most important treasure I have is Jesus. He is my life—He is my everything. My second treasure of course is my husband and my children. My heart just spills over with gratitude to the Lord for giving me such an amazing family, they are precious. Third is this ministry. I treasure this ministry because having the privilege and the honor of sharing the Gospel is the absolute desire of my heart. There are many days when I can hardly believe the Lord has blessed my life in this way. I am able to do what I love, which is to be a wife, mother *and* encourage others to deepen their relationship with Jesus. I believe I've won the lottery without even buying a ticket!

However ask this question when the kids are arguing, the dog has tracked mud on the carpet, and my husband has called to tell me he's bringing people home for dinner . . . in fifteen minutes! Then the answer might be very different. All kidding aside, actually my answer wouldn't change a bit. Jesus is my ultimate treasure.

Wright

Well, what a great conversation. I really appreciate this time you've spent with me this afternoon; it's been enlightening for me and very, very interesting.

Vopat

Well thank you, David. I have really enjoyed this opportunity to speak with you and share a little bit about my life and In His Grace Ministries.

Wright

Today we've been talking with Lonna Vopat who is a nationally known ministry speaker and television talk show host. Others have said that the Lord has blessed Lonna with being able to communicate His word with boldness, compassion, and humor. I think we've found out that whoever said that knew what they were talking about, or at least they knew a whole lot about Lonna.

Thank you so much for being with us today on *Speaking of Faith*.

Vopat

Thank you again, David, and God bless you.

About The Author

LONNA VOPAT is the founder of In His Grace Ministries as well as the host of the television talk show *Between Friends*. Her ministry has taken her across the Untied States and internationally. Her passion for the Word of God has been shared on Christian radio and television throughout the nation. She and her family live in north central Idaho where they enjoy the outdoors and raising horses. Lonna is a member of the Church of the Nazarene, where she is involved in youth and women's ministry.

Lonna Vopat
In His Grace Ministries
P.O. Box 95 Grangeville, ID 83530
www.in-his-grace.com

Chapter 7

PAT MAYFIELD

David Wright (Wright)

Today, we welcome Pat Mayfield, president of Pat Mayfield Consulting, LLC. Pat is a successful business consultant, professional trainer, and accomplished speaker. Audiences especially enjoy the practical advice she presents with real life examples, personal experiences, and humor. Pat's background includes successfully working with multi-million and trillion-dollar businesses to grow their sales and increase profits. Pat's specialties include leadership, sales and negotiating, protocol, and customer service. She holds BS, MA, and MBA degrees, has authored four business books, and co-authored *Leadership Defined* and *Conversations on Success.*

Pat, welcome to *Speaking of Faith.*

Pat Mayfield (Mayfield)

Thanks, David. As always, it's a pleasure to talk with you.

Wright

When we first became acquainted, you indicated an interest in contributing to a book on faith. Why is faith important to you?

Mayfield

My interest in a book on faith is both personal and professional. Faith has long been an important part of my personal life and when I joined the business world, faith became a major factor in my professional life as well. In business and in life, clear-cut answers are not always apparent; sometimes a final action is determined simply on faith. Faith plays a major role in decision-making, building relationships, and even long-term planning. It is not unusual for my faith to affect a decision, influence a client or colleague relationship, or become part of my company strategy and vision.

I think sharing one's faith is part of the responsibility of having faith, and this interview is a wonderful opportunity to share some unusual and unexpected situations in which faith played a part. It's easy to have faith during the good times, but I'm not sure how one gets through the challenges of life and work without faith. For many years my favorite slogan and greatest motivator has been the phrase *"keep the faith."* When everything else has been thought out, discussed, or tried, it often comes down to keeping the faith. This powerful phrase is a great reminder that faith is like the best of best friends—always there, anytime, and anywhere.

When you called to let me know this book would feature Dr. Robert Schuller, I was absolutely thrilled. For many, many years, I have watched Dr. Schuller's televised weekly "Hour of Power" in the Crystal Cathedral. Having moved numerous times all over the United States, one of the few consistencies in my life was the "Hour of Power;" always on at the same time, same place, every week. Even though I would be involved in formal churches, Dr. Schuller's message through his sermons and books was an important part in my keeping the faith and keeping grounded as we were constantly uprooted.

For years, I have read his books and given them as gifts. My favorite is *Tough Times Never Last, But Tough People Do.* The real-life stories of those who overcame truly difficult circumstances in life make this book a classic for encouragement. Also, when corporations began downsizing as a way to increase profits, this book served as an inspiration to many going through the tough time of losing their jobs.

Dr. Schuller has created many long lasting memories for me. When I started my company in 2000, I often found encouragement in remembering how Dr. Schuller began his first preaching assignment at a drive-in movie theater! Another great memory is the way Dr. Schuller greets the congregation of the Crystal Cathedral each Sunday with, "This is the day the Lord hath made, Let us rejoice and be glad in it" (Psalm 118:24). When Dr. Schuller says it with his special positive passion, one cannot help but smile and refocus on this one day.

Wright
When did you first relate faith to the business world and how has that impacted your career?

Mayfield
My first jobs out of college were in the public non-profit sector and were geared to education and giving to others. It was through a chance meeting on an airplane that I entered the corporate world. Although I was told I would be trained, somehow time and geographical separation just didn't permit that to happen. This first business assignment was as a manufacturer's representative in the gift industry. It didn't take long to figure out that I needed my own system and a philosophy that would work for both my customers and me.

One of the greatest bits of advice I received from a competitor that first year was to always protect my own name. Companies would come and go, but my name would always stay. It was because of this comment that I decided to use the simple but significant Golden Rule theory. I would simply treat my customers as I would want to be treated, i.e., ethically and with courtesy and respect. The Golden Rule can be found in Matthew 7:12 and Luke 6:31.

Years later, while working as a sales executive in the corporate world, I experienced a difficult situation with a retailer and its customer. It was the worst situation of Murphy's Law I ever experienced. My company was in the wrong—not on purpose, but because of a major miscommunication. The customer of this Midwestern retailer, who was a vice president in a national corporation, had ordered products worth thousands of dollars for his home.

The first issue was that our product didn't arrive when we said it would. We said we would ship it on a certain date, but didn't. When the retailer finally received the shipment, the product had defects and some of the items were broken. Our company was known for our high quality in both product and service, so this truly was an unusual situation. Most issues could be resolved with one phone call to the factory, but not in this case. No matter what the factory told me would happen, it didn't. It was a nightmare for the retailer, the customer, and me. I apologized to the retailer and the customer over and over. I sent both of them candy. I apologized more. I sent both of them flowers. Nothing helped because they did not get the product when they needed it. I was greatly humbled by this experience.

During this episode, I typed out the store name of the retailer and the last name of the customer and taped it on the back of my nameplate. Then, when people would sit across the desk from me and compliment our product or our work, they could see my name on the nameplate in my office, but what I saw on the backside of the nameplate was the name of the retailer and the customer that we let down. No matter how good we thought we were and wanted to be, at least two people had been disappointed. I still have that nameplate as a reminder of the power of the Golden Rule and the importance of treating others as I want to be treated.

Wright

I understand you were a part of a *Faith in the Workplace* program during your corporate years. Tell us more about that.

Mayfield

Yes, that was such a special time in my life. I was living in Princeton and working close by at a corporation's national headquarters. I was asked by the leadership of the Nassau Presbyterian Church (a beautiful, historical, stately church in the center of Princeton) if I would be interested in helping with a new *Faith in the Workplace* program. I was excited to be a part of this new program that emphasized faith and career. It provided an opportunity to connect and share with others who were facing similar work circumstances and challenges.

Pat Kidd, who also worked for a large corporation, and associate church minister Cindy Jarvis, originated the idea for this program. At the first meeting, held on a cold Saturday morning, fifteen business leaders gathered to help formulate the goals and objectives of the program. A great deal of time was spent on introductions as each person shared his or her situation and the challenges of the connection of faith and work.

Stories were similar around the room: people versus profit, short-term versus long-term decisions, balancing family with the long hours required for business leadership, and early retirement versus fulfilling life-long career dreams. The most significant challenge for everyone around the table was making the right decision and doing the right thing in the midst of adversaries and naysayers. Most shared the belief that if one has faith, a high level of integrity and ethics is required in decision-making.

The program was truly successful. I was always amazed at how many high level executives would attend these early Saturday morning sessions. Not only did the Saturday morning meetings continue, but public seminars on a variety of topics were also organized by the *Faith in the Workplace* leadership.

During the early months of the program, David Miller, a former senior executive in the financial world, became involved. At that time David was attending the Theological Seminary in Princeton. His strong leadership and passion, coupled with Pat Kidd's energy and vision, took this program to new levels. With the support of the church, Pat and David sponsored several business- and faith-oriented seminars open to the public with great success—the attendance far exceeded expectations.

Since my move to California to start my company, I've watched the impact that David continues to make on the world of faith in the workplace. After graduating with a Master of Divinity and a Ph.D. in Ethics from Princeton Theological Seminary, Dr. Miller co-founded the Avodah Institute, working with CEOs who seek to integrate the claims of their faith with the demands of their work. Avodah in Hebrew means *worship and work*. David was then asked to take the work of the Avodah to Yale Divinity School and serve as executive director of the newly founded Yale Center for Faith and Culture (www.yale.edu/faith). The Center's mission is to promote the practice of faith in all spheres of life through theological research and leadership development with key emphasis on ethics and spiritually in the workplace. We were so lucky to have the leadership of Pat Kidd and Dr. Miller to guide this program.

Wright

I understand you have a program called *Making Time for Your Soul*. What is that program about?

Mayfield

This program actually came out of one of the *Faith in the Workplace* meetings. During that particular meeting, we went around the room and each person shared his or her own challenges with balancing personal and professional life. I was amazed at the number of highly successful people who shared their regrets in life. My philosophy has always been to have no regrets. We cannot look back and wish we could do it over . . . we cannot change history. What we can change is how we act and react in the future. Rather than dwell on the unchangeable, it's critical that we forgive or let go and that we spend our energy and efforts on the positive for the future. The ability to forgive and forget while learning from the past is a critical part of living a full life. A life partially lived in the past is a life partially lived.

Because so many felt they had made wrong decisions, especially personal decisions during complex work situations, I created the program *Making Time for Your Soul*. This is a four-hour time management seminar which focuses on how to define the spiritual aspect of daily life and create a schedule that recognizes and honors spiritual needs.

Many people have faith, but in the midst of complexity and challenge, sometimes it may be hard to draw upon that faith, especially if faith is only an occasional friend. The more we keep the faith, the more the faith keeps us.

Wright

How have people influenced your faith?

Mayfield

Numerous people of faith come to mind. Sometimes people influence us in ways without ever knowing it. During a tough personal time, a book I read frequently was, *The Power of Positive Thinking,* by Norman Vincent Peale. While preparing for a business meeting in Los Angeles, I pulled this book from my bookshelf to read on the plane. I had not read the book in years, but was truly reassured by the repeating premise of Philippians 4:13, "I can do all things which strengthen me." To this day, it's a favorite scripture.

I had been reading this book a lot, when I looked at the inside cover and saw the inscription signature. The book had been a gift from a dear friend from college, Ron Robinson. Knowing that this wonderful friend had given me the book made its contents even more significant. Ron is a generous person—probably one of the most generous individuals I've ever known— and a master of encouragement through his thousands of handwritten notes to friends and colleagues.

Another special friend is Captain Bill Ryan, a New York fireman, whom I met several months after September 11, 2001. I met Billy at a New York Rotary Club meeting where I was presenting a check for the 9/11 Rotary Fund from the Pleasanton North Rotary Club to the

New York City Rotary Club. I was seated next to Billy at the meeting and in the course of conversation shared that my dad had been a fireman during part of his career. When you've been reared in the world of the fire department, the bond of the families of all firefighters is beyond description.

After the meeting, Billy offered to help me get off at the correct exit from the subway to get to the platform at Ground Zero. As we got close to the subway stop, rather than telling me, he actually got off the subway with me. Because he was dressed in the fireman's dress uniform, the other NYC firemen there allowed us to go through Fire Station Number 10, which is at the base of Ground Zero. As we stood there on the top of the fire station, we were in total silence. Words cannot express the disbelief, the intensity of the emotions, the frustrations, and the incredible sadness I felt. After several minutes of silent observation, Billy helped me to get a cab and then he headed home to Staten Island.

Billy and I have kept in touch by e-mail and we've been able to visit during my occasional trips back to New York. Billy shared how his faith kept him going through the most difficult times of 9/11.

The first story is about the *power of the child*—Billy's granddaughter, Hailey. Hailey, born July 30, 2001, and her mom, Samantha, were living with Billy and his wife, Sue. In the days and weeks after 9/11 many of Billy's firefighter friends, after a long day at Ground Zero, would gather at Billy and Sue's home. The friends came not only to be with Billy and the Ryan family, but especially to be near baby Hailey. The main request from many of his friends was to hold baby Hailey.

Holding Hailey seemed to bring some sense of peacefulness to the exhausted firefighters after the long hours dealing with all of the losses and horrific effects of 9/11 and the challenges of working at Ground Zero. As Billy describes it, being around a six-week-old baby helped to bring back the hope of life and the faith in goodness. (The power of Captain Ryan and his granddaughter Hailey was featured in the 9/11 issue of *Time* magazine and also in the book, *Stepping Through the Ashes,* by Eugene Richards.)

The second touching story of faith is about the *power of a song*. One of Billy's favorite church songs "Here I Am Lord" kept coming back to him as the rubble of the World Trade Center surrounded him on 9/11. Billy shared that thinking of the words and just humming that song over and over in his mind kept him filled with faith and most of all, with hope. The power of that one hymn remains an incredible connection to his faith.

Finding faith during difficult times can be hard. Although Billy's experiences could fill a book, Billy's personal faith during trauma and tragedy is an inspiration to me.

Before starting my company in California, I had the good fortune to work in the corporate world with leaders of faith. In my last corporate position I worked for a company that had two exceptional executives—both were men of faith.

Rich Stearns, then the CEO of the company, kept the largest Bible I have ever seen open on his desk. His faith not only was public, it was truly an open book. Rich left the corporate world to become President and CEO of World Vision U.S. where he continues today.

Bill Bracy, who was President of the company at that time, was extremely active in The Church of Jesus Christ of Latter-day Saints in New Jersey. Bill went on to be the President and COO of Bell Sports and later the CEO of Lionel Trains where he recently retired.

Being able to work with these two executives of great faith was an inspiration. They were wonderful leaders and a blessing to the company. They set the example of true leadership of faith in the workplace.

My mother-in-law, Helene Mayfield (who passed away several years ago) had the strongest faith of anyone I've ever personally known. She was an incredible woman of great spiritual faith. Just being around her was enough to feel her strong sense of soul and faith; you could almost see her genuine faith through her eyes. Her great spirit was evident years ago when only six months after she had open-heart surgery, she was riding camels in the Holy Land! She was a special woman and a generous mother-in-law. Although life situations separated us for many years, the memory of her strong faith and character still is in my heart.

Several of my close friends have also been an inspiration as they live their daily lives in faith. Maynette and Dave Breithaupt and Judy and Dennis Matthies were instrumental in introducing me into their church family. Being neighbors and walking partners, Judy and I spent many hours sharing stories of faith during our early morning exercise walks. Elizabeth Hamrick also plays an important role in the discussion of many faith-based business decisions. Carol Ott-Olson was the first person to ask me to attend her church in my new location. This act of kindness was the beginning of a long-term friendship. And for many years my dear friend, Misty Tyree, and I have spent hours thinking and talking through faith-based choices in life and in work.

Wright

Are there any companies or organizations that have influenced or impacted your faith?

Mayfield

Anytime a person of faith is working with another person or company of faith, it makes a difference. The differences are not generally discussed, but it is quietly and mutually understood that true faith will yield deserved trust, quality, and mutual benefit.

David, your company Insight Publishing has truly been a blessing to me. To work with your faith-based organization has been a wonderful experience and has provided special opportunities I would have never had if our paths had not crossed. The excitement of opening the first box of books in the first shipment to me is indescribable. The books are like adding members to one's family. I shall ever be grateful for that first phone call I received from your company and for the relationships with everyone in your organization.

Another company that has special meaning to me and to many others is the California-based In-N-Out Burger chain. The In-N-Out Burger was the first drive-through hamburger stand in California. Their original philosophy in 1948 of providing the freshest and highest quality ingredients, cleanliness, friendliness, and a tasty end product is still in effect today.

My son introduced me to their great hamburger while I was living in New Jersey, so whenever I was in California, I would always try to have an In-N-Out burger while in town. Now that I live in California, I really get to enjoy. David, it really is a great hamburger!

What I didn't learn until later is that a scripture (such as John 3:16) is placed on the bottom of the beverage cup, and another scripture is typed on the edge of the hamburger wrapper. Although the company does not publicize this—not even on their Web site—the scriptures are known and discussed by word of mouth. How nice to know a company that produces such high quality is also a company of faith.

Wright

The Bible is a great source of inspiration. Do you have special scriptures that inspire you?

Mayfield

Yes, and I think that is one of the greatest benefits of the Bible. Although I cannot remember every story in the Bible, there are certain scriptures that have had special meaning during special times. My favorites scriptures are, "For God so loved the world, He gave his only begotten Son, that whoever believes in him should not perish but have eternal life" (John 3:16), "So faith, hope, love abide, these three; but the greatest of these is love" (I Corinthians 13:13), and as I mentioned before, "I can do all things through Christ which strengthen me" (Philippians 4:13). I also truly enjoy reading the beatitudes (Matthew 5:3–11). My sister-in-law, Judy Rotenberry, sent me a flier on the explanation of The Twenty-Third Psalm from, *God's Psychiatry,* by Charles L. Allen, which I treasure. I have this and other favorite scriptures I love to read collected in my *Scriptbook for the Soul.*

Wright

What is this *Scriptbook* you've developed?

Mayfield

The *Scriptbook for the Soul*—like a scrapbook for scriptures—was created for the *Making Time for Your Soul* program. Because life becomes so full and so complex, I wanted to create a personalized, condensed collection that can help bring one back to basic beliefs. I call it the *Scriptbook for Your Soul.* Mine is a collection of favorite scriptures and verses that have special meaning to me and I also include special notes, cards and letters, photos, and even postcards that are reminders of significant occurrences.

For example, one of the greatest sights of human love and respect for faith I have ever witnessed is captured in a postcard of the Shrine of Our Lady of Guadalupe in Mexico City.

While on vacation, I happened to be at the Shrine when hundreds of pilgrims arrived in school buses that were decorated in colorful paper flowers and crepe paper streamers. When the pilgrims got off the buses, they immediately went to their knees. While still on their knees, they lit candles and then proceeded with heads lowered in prayer to the shrine of the Lady of Guadalupe. They walked on their knees the entire distance to pay homage to the Lady of Guadalupe. The bus drop-off point was a very long distance from the entrance to the Shrine. Many were people with disabilities and making their journey from the bus to the Shrine was a physical challenge.

The short version of the story about the Lady is that on December 9, 1531, a vision, described as a "Lady from Heaven," appeared to Juan Diego a few miles north of Mexico City. The lady in his vision identified herself as the Virgin Mary, the Mother of the True God. Juan, a poor Aztec, was instructed by the Lady to have the bishop build a temple on the site where she appeared. Since the bishop initially did not believe Juan, he challenged Juan numerous times for proof. The bishop finally believed this vision was real when a painting of the vision of the Lady was found imprinted on Juan's tilma (rectangular cape). Because this cape was made of poor quality, cactus cloth experts thought it would deteriorate within twenty years, but the image on the cloth is still miraculously there today. And yes, the Shrine was finally completed in 1709.

Another item in the Scriptbook is a photo of a fallen tree that I took from the second floor in my Princeton townhouse. That year had held many difficult and unexpected personal and professional challenges. This particular day, after hearing a very loud thump (I mean really *loud*), I ran to the second story window to look out on the street. Much to my surprise, I saw a flattened forty-foot tree that had just landed in the only vacant area of grass across the street. It was a miracle the buildings on either side of the fallen tree were not touched. The tree barely missed two cars parked close by.

The tree had fallen during a Nor'easter and if it had landed on the opposite side, it would have taken my townhouse down. Many of the neighbors who were aware of my challenges that year gathered outside in amazement at the "luck" of where the tree landed. I really took that tree landing as a sign that the "bad" stuff in my life was over. I still call it the Angel tree. For me, it was a great sign of hope.

Wright

Pat, speaking of prayer, how important is prayer to you?

Mayfield

Prayer is part of the communication of faith. For me, prayer is to the soul as vitamins are to health. When I was a kid growing up in Mabelvale, Arkansas, we had Wednesday night prayer meetings at the Baseline Baptist Church. So prayer was a part of my childhood routine.

The most powerful example of the power of prayer I personally witnessed early in life was when Susie Owens Shumaker's husband, Dale (known as "Bud" to many of his friends), was in a life-changing accident. Susie and Bud had recently moved to Austin, Texas, to join Bud's brother in his landscaping business. Susie and Dale had been married for five years and their daughter, Karen, was approaching her second birthday when tragedy struck.

While working, the dump truck Dale was driving suddenly flipped over on a curve in the road. The injury he sustained was described by doctors as a severe twisting of the brain stem. Although his vital signs were strong, Dale had no movement in one arm or either leg. The doctors said there were no signs of Dale waking up and he had a high fever, which was of great concern.

On the Sunday afternoon after the accident, with little hope, Susie could not just sit back and wait. She contacted both her church minister in Austin, where the family was living, as well as her home church in Little Rock, and asked for Dale and his family to be added to their prayer lists. Well, not only did both ministers add Dale to the list, both ministers in these two different states took the full Sunday evening service of ministry to pray for Dale. That very night, Dale's fever finally broke.

This was just one of many steps forward needed for Dale. Dale lay in an unconscious state with serious head injuries for six weeks. The prognosis was still not good. Dale could not speak, nor could he use either leg or one of his arms.

The prayers continued. Not only did both churches pray, but prayer groups in other churches also added Dale to their prayer lists and new prayer groups were formed for Dale's continuous improvement. Susie continued to encourage prayer wherever she could. As the months went by Dale and Susie learned that prayer groups for Dale had been formed all over the country.

When Dale finally did recover, he essentially had to start life all over again, learning to walk, talk, eat, feed himself, and perform basic tasks such as reading and math. It was going to be a long road ahead. But neither Susie nor Dale lost their faith. In fact, the prayers and support of their church community seem to strengthen them more than ever before.

Dale and Susie credit the power of prayer for Dale's survival. For those of us on the praying side, we were profoundly affected by this obvious power of prayer. Susie's strength during this crisis is also a life-long memory of the power of faith.

Wright

As a person of faith, have you had any unusual experiences in your life you would like to share?

Mayfield

David, there have been several moments in my life during a crisis when I was overcome for just a few moments by a total feeling of warmth, peace, and contentment. The best way for me to describe this experience is that it felt like soft, large wings embracing me for a few moments. Even though this state lasted only a few moments, it was if I was being surrounded by great invisible love. Somehow I knew that when this cloak surrounded me everything would work out—that everything would be all right.

There are two memorable times. Once was when my town home complex in Princeton caught fire. The minute I got into my hotel room (the Hyatt agreed to house the residents of the ten units that night without charge), I dropped to my knees and prayed in thanks that no one had died in the fire, which had taken numerous fire departments hours to put out. The fire had started close to midnight, but it was not until three thirty in the morning that I felt I could leave the complex.

When I returned to the complex the next morning, a feeling of peace and contentment came over me. It was at that moment I knew we would be able to recover and that it would take around a year to rebuild. It was almost exactly one year that the building units were reconstructed and the issues connected to the fire were resolved.

Although this was not the first time I had experienced these feelings, it was one of the more intense and reassuring. There was absolutely no doubt in my mind we would survive this ordeal, which became a most complex situation. This sense of hope was especially important to me as I was serving as president of the Homeowners Association that year.

Another significant time was in the fall of 1998 after I fell and severely injured both feet. I was lying in the hospital awaiting surgery and truly wondering when and if the angels would visit me with their cloak of encouragement. Because I had experienced the angels several times unexpectedly before, now I was hoping and counting on their embrace. It was almost eleven hours before the surgical room was available, so I had hours of lying on the gurney. But finally, it did come and once again I knew I would be okay.

David, these unusual moments cannot be controlled and I can only hope for the reassurance, but I'm so grateful that I've been able to have peace of mind during times of crises. To go from feeling anxious to total peace within seconds is beyond the powers of the body. These moments truly reinforce my faith and remind me to always...*keep the faith.*

About The Author

PAT MAYFIELD is the president of Pat Mayfield Consulting, LLC, which is a business consulting company with a national-client base. She is an accomplished speaker, professional trainer, and successful business consultant. The company, which began in mid-2000, specializes in consulting and training in leadership, sales, negotiating, customer service, and protocol.

Pat is the author of *Giving and Getting: Tips on Negotiating; Business Tips and Techniques, Manners for Success®, Please Don't Drink from the Finger Bowl!™*, and is a contributing author to *Leadership Defined and Conversations on Success.*

Pat is classified as a Professional Speaker by the National Speakers Association. She holds a BS from the University of Arkansas, an MA from Columbia University and an MBA from St. Mary's College.

Pat Mayfield
Pat Mayfield Consulting, LLC
P.O. Box 10095
Pleasanton, CA 94588
Phone: 925.600.0584
E-mail: pat@patmayfield.com
www.patmayfield.com

Chapter 8

ANN JILLIAN

David E. Wright (Wright)

Today, we're talking with Ann Jillian—three-time Emmy nominee and Golden Globe Award-winning actress. In addition to being a motivational speaker, Ann is an accomplished performer in all areas of show business. She is a star of motion pictures, television, nightclubs, and the Broadway stage. She was voted one of the most admired women of the world in *Good Housekeeping Magazine*'s 1990 poll.

She is a volunteer performer for the St. Vincent Meals on Wheels program to feed the elderly, and she is a lifetime board member of the American Cancer Society and St. Jude Children's Hospital. Ann also works for the USO, the Disabled American Veterans Hospital visiting program, and many other charities.

In 1988, Ann won the Golden Globe Best Actress award for her starring role in the poignant NBC television biography, *The Ann Jillian Story*, which recounted her victory over breast cancer. Ann's motivational lectures are filled with humor, music, and information about life, health, and the joys of being a mom.

Ann Jillian, welcome to *Speaking of Faith*!

Ann Jillian (Jillian)

Thank you so much for having me here.

Wright

Miss Jillian, most of our readers have seen you on television but may not be familiar with your background. Would you tell us how you started in the entertainment business?

Jillian

Actually, it has been more years ago than I care to remember. My mother, God love her, was an old-fashioned Lithuanian lady. When I was around four years old, we were living in Cambridge, Massachusetts, which is where I was born. My mother was watching me perform in a civic function that we had there in Cambridge. Some kids did some piano things, others did some poetic presentations, and I sang. When the music stopped, I didn't. I kept going. A man who was probably the size of Mickey Rooney, now that I think of it— although to me he was pretty big—came and took me off stage. My mother was in the wings, and she said, "Ah ha! We go to Hollywood!" So she uprooted the entire family and brought us to Hollywood.

I was discovered by coincidence. I know God had His hand in this plan somewhere. A letter came to the school that I was attending. It was from Art Linkletter's *House Party*. They gave it to the principal, who then chose a teacher, who then chose four children to be on the show. So I was on one of the original episodes of *Kids Say the Darndest Things*.

During that time, my mom met another mom who had an agent for her child. The woman suggested that we should do that, so my mom found an agent, and from that point on, I was in *Babes in Toyland, Gypsy*, and a number of other things.

I went through a transitional period where I kind of held back and kept going to school. Then I reemerged as an adult in Chicago in something called *Goodnight Ladies,* where I did meet Mr. Mickey Rooney. He was about to start *Sugar Babies*, and he told the producers about me. I auditioned for the producers, and I got the superette lead. So my husband and I went to Broadway.

After our time on Broadway we came back to Los Angeles and started with *It's a Living* and the rest of those credits that you gave. I ended up with twenty-seven films under my belt and numerous specials. That's how it started out.

Wright

That's interesting. I'm going to go to the video store and check out the Natalie Wood version of *Gypsy* and try to find you.

Jillian

I played June. There are two versions of June, and I played the older one. There's also Louise—the part that Natalie played—who later becomes Gypsy. I was Natalie's sister.

Wright

In their early years, most successful people in any profession develop a strong sense of purpose and dedicate themselves to certain tasks or actions that will lead to specific results. What things did you do or what personal characteristics did you develop to ensure your success?

Jillian

It kind of unfolded, you know. It wasn't in my mind, as I recall. In fact, I was still searching. My mother had it her mind what I was going to do, because she felt that what I had was a natural God-given talent. God was big in our house. She felt that it would be wrong not to develop those areas. Did I actually have an interest in them and think, "Oh, this is my goal"? No, I don't believe I did. I was just a good girl, and I figured Mama *did* know best, and Dad worked toward that end.

It was probably somewhere around the time that I became an adolescent when I looked at my parents—I saw how hard they worked and I thought to myself, "What am I going to do? What are my strengths?" I kept hearing people say that in order to really have success, you must do what you love and what you do naturally. So I saw that my mother was actually quite right. I did, in fact, enjoy presenting a story in front of a camera and I did enjoy singing, so I thought, "All right, this is what I'm going to do."

I'm a relatively shy person, believe it or not, so I worked to counteract that shyness. I knew that it was not going to be a benefit to me if I were going into this business. This business, I knew, was something that would afford me the ability to take care of my parents later on in life, because they are my family. Believe it or not, it was not a self-oriented thing. My goal was not to be a star; but my goal was to be a working actress who could help my family.

Wright

Did they live long enough to enjoy your successes?

Jillian

Yes, thank goodness. You know, I have always prayed. Early on in my life, I remember going to a party after high school. One young man happened to be saying something about God answering prayers. I found myself listening to this individual, who said, "Oh come on. You don't believe that God really answers your prayers." Something— and I don't know where it came from—compelled me. I heard myself saying, "Sure, He does. He answers your prayers even if He says no." I realized at that moment how much I believed that God listens to us and God is there for us.

Everything I ever prayed for about my parents, He took care of. In their golden years I wanted them to not have to go through the pain of seeing their child debilitated by cancer. And the good Lord helped to restore me in that particular area.

I then became pregnant. It was almost like He gave me a stamp of approval after fifteen years of childless marriage. So seven years after my breast cancer, I had a child—my one and only son. And then I prayed, "Please, God, let my parents be able to know him, that he would be old enough to remember them. And He did." So all the way down the line, it was really other-oriented. I knew that this was what He gave me to work with and that this was what I must go after. So I continued. That was my goal—to take care of my family.

Everything I did, I did basically because I knew that I had to. If I was shy, if I was scared, if I was nervous about going out on stage, I would say a prayer ahead of time. I would offer it up to Him, and then I would say to myself, "You have to do this, because there is no other way that you will be able to take care of them the way you want to." So I went out there, and I did it. Each job was a step to the next, and I literally learned on the job.

Wright

How did your relationship with God affect your career choices along the way?

Jillian

It was a very conscious choice that I made—when I was able to be in that position to make choices—to choose projects that had hopeful endings or that had hopeful feelings throughout. A lot of them were true stories.

Wright

Neither my wife nor I will admit to it, but we are hooked on a television show called *Inside the Actors Studio*.

Jillian

Yes.

Wright

And that is the recurring theme with all the famous actors that are on that show. At first, you have to do anything and everything anybody asks you, but then you get your own choice of scripts. That must be wonderful when you get to that point.

Jillian

It's funny, because everybody is at his or her own level. I won't get, and didn't get—much to my dismay—the scripts that perhaps Meryl Streep or Sally Field or any number of other actresses at that time got. But in my area, what I got was abundant enough. And I figured if they were coming to me, God wanted me to make choices, and I did make the choices. I hope that they were in accordance with what He wanted me to do. I also had a few scripts (more than a few) that came to my door and I said, "Absolutely not. Why would you think that I would do that?"

Wright

When I talked to Jennifer O'Neill last month, I found that her Christian beliefs cost her a lot in her career, especially the Hollywood part of it. She was on *The View* some time ago, I think. She took a stand against abortion, and the other four or five ladies on the show said that they were really angry and that Jennifer could never appear on *The View* again.

Jillian

What?

Wright

But the network started getting phone calls saying that Jennifer O'Neill was great and that they agreed with her, so they asked her back. *The View* asked her back after saying she would never appear there again. So she's taken some heat for her Christian beliefs.

Jillian

Well, God love her! And I know that He does, because she's out there upholding His will. I'll tell you what, we are all one day going to meet our Maker, and we all will be held responsible for His will. That's the way I feel, obviously, so there you go.

Wright

Good Housekeeping Magazine named you as one of the most admired women in the world. Of course, to me and others, that's really impressive, especially when you consider other women who hold that distinction. As a shy person, how did that make you feel?

Jillian

I was very honored, because if you take a look at that year and the women with whom I shared that honor, I did not see myself in the league of someone like a Mother Teresa. There were other women who were in serious areas of politics and so forth. These were women who were quite accomplished. So for me to be put in the same league was a tremendous honor. I believe that others saw things inside of the things that I was doing. I would imagine that it was probably because of the way I handled the breast cancer. It was probably more about how I continued a mission to remind women of the importance of early detection and swift medical action. I think that those two things probably elevated how people perceived me in that respect; but I was and am still quite honored—very honored—and I will always remain quite surprised that I was voted in that way.

Wright

I watched my wife go through a struggle with colorectal cancer for two years, and she finally made it through. Everyone, including me, thought she would not. We hoped that she would and prayed that she would, but there were a few times when I doubted. So trust me, you really *do* deserve the honor.

Jillian

The honor is shared, because everybody that has to go through that kind of a challenge—a cancer challenge or any kind of a life-threatening or a life-altering illness—has to come up to the plate. They have to live through this, so anything that I endured is only representative of all those silent heroes nobody knows about because they don't make their living in front of a camera. I happened to, and perhaps that is what placed me in that position; but I share that with your wife. I share it with all the people—all the ladies, our daughters, our aunts, our sisters, our wives, and the wives throughout the world—who have ever had to go through that.

Wright

Will you tell us about your struggle with cancer and how it immediately affected your life?

Jillian

Cancer is a family thing. It is a struggle that everybody in their own way has to go through once it hits one person in the family.

I was raised in a very religious family, a faith-filled family. When I developed cancer, it validated my beliefs. The things I learned through catechism and through my early years I had to pull up and out of me and use as my anchor. And the cancer actually validated everything that I was taught to believe—the idea that every single second of life is worth living; the idea that life is sacred from the very beginning to the very end; that our good Lord is really in charge; that many things I believed became validated by that experience.

An interesting thing occurred. I was a compassionate person beforehand, both intellectually and in my heart, but when I developed cancer and walked through the fears, walked through the challenges, walked through the treatments and the sufferings that I endured, my compassion became an extremely deep one. All of a sudden, I was united with the sufferings of all of humanity.

I had people who sent me letters from around the world, telling me about their own experiences. And I literally had to take time off from the hours that I spent reading at home after the surgery, because it took my breath away. I so deeply felt their struggles and their sufferings, and it really takes what you have on the surface to a very deep level.

I feel that there was growth in it. You know, there were many dark days that my family and I had to endure and, obviously, cancer is not a good thing—anything that is life-threatening like that is not a good thing. But like the mythological phoenix rising from the ashes, something does become resurrected in a time like that. It is this spirit—the human spirit—and it facilitates the ability to grow. Those kinds of challenges facilitate the ability to grow, and that is *always* a good thing.

Wright

My wife and I were in a meeting a while ago with several people at church. We were discussing hardships and things that people had gone through. My wife made the statement, as you just said, that even though cancer is horrible and even though the pain and all the suffering is terrible, she would not give anything for having gone through the experience. And I almost thought she was nuts, but as I looked at her, I could tell she was dead serious.

Jillian

I understand her. It is not something that you would wish on any-one or yourself, but in the throes of it, you can only look upon it to see what redemptive value it has. There is inherent in all of our struggles a redemptive value, and obviously, God, who is in all parts of our lives, every day of our lives, wanted us to glean from it what we could.

My suffering was, all of a sudden, united with the suffering of eve-rybody—of all of mankind—in various different ways, because I felt close to that suffering.

It also became very clear that I could not sit and complain about it, because my suffering was elevated to Christ's suffering, and that made my suffering sacred, because at that moment on the cross, He elevated all of mankind's suffering. Up until that time, we didn't know why we did. In our minds, in our hearts, we thought, "How on earth could this suffering possibly mean something good?" And yet, out of that horrific death on that cross, He made it a source of salva-tion for all of us. So I looked at that. I thought to myself, "There's nothing that I can suffer here that can be more than what He suf-fered there." So that helped me get through it.

Wright

My wife and my family were absolutely overwhelmed and over-come by all of the prayers and acts of kindness that were directed toward us during those times. I couldn't help but say that it was, in some way, modeling what Christ did to have that much kindness. I have never asked anybody for anything, but boy, I tell you what, people just started helping and doing things and calling and writing. And people were praying around the world. There were stories of churches of 5,000 and 6,000 people getting together in Guatemala and other places and praying for her. It was unbelievable. Did you experience that sort of thing?

Jillian

Yes! Yes! It was an amazing, amazing phenomenon. Within the first week, we had 60,000 letters. Over the course of time, I'm sure it went up to somewhere around 300,000 letters. But I got the prayers. I had people from Israel sending me prayers, and they had cedar trees planted in my name. And you know that this is a godly thing that happens. I wept. I spent a lot of time weeping, because I was so totally stunned and so totally touched by what came through. You're right, it's a magnificent thing to see how the spirit of so many people will come up and help—it reaches out to help others.

Wright

How much of your recovery do you think was an act of faith?

Jillian

To me, *everything* is connected, so I have to say 100 percent. I keep coming back to faith, because to me, He is the source of all good. So whatever recovery came to me came through the hands, minds, and instruments of those people through whom He works.

We are His instruments if we are open to it. It's like ripples. Somebody throws a pebble in a still lake, and you see the ripples going out. Some people are out in the community, and they are compelled by their inner selves to do something for the community. Some are more vocal; some work just through writing. It doesn't matter how, but we all ripple out into our extended families—into our communities, the nation, the world. It comes through an inspiration, I believe, and that inspiration to me is God. He works through His people—our doctors, our nurses, our researchers, and everybody. They are touched by God. They are kissed by God, and they are commissioned by that kiss to go out and fulfill a mission that only they can fulfill.

Some of us are listening; some of us are not. Some of us may hear well early on in life, and some may find it by stumbling and perhaps by talking with others. But we cannot stop talking. We cannot stop writing. We cannot stop living in the example that He wants us to live.

But to get back to the point, let me say I believe that faith is the anchor. Faith is what everything is built upon. If I could give anything to my son, it would be the gift of introducing him to a strong faith and then weaving it into each and every single part of his daily life. I am a Christian. I am Roman Catholic. To me, it's not just something that I do every Sunday when I go to mass. My faith has become a part of my very identity. My birth name is Ann Jura Nauseda. Ann Murcia is my married name, and Ann Jillian is my professional name, but whatever name I have, I am this woman of faith, which is a part of every fiber of my being.

My Catholicism is a part of me and my very identity. I cannot extricate myself from that. It's who I am, and having that strength gives me strength of purpose. It lights how I see things in life, and it helps to light the decisions that I am going to make in life. The one thing that we have—and I can be very happy in talking about it as far as the Christian faith is concerned—is that when we are knocked down to our knees, we are able to get up again. We do get knocked down on our knees—nobody is perfect. The only One who was perfect died on the cross on that Good Friday. But we are able once again, with that faith, to breathe in, think of our Lord, and move on ahead. That is the gift that I wanted to give to my son.

Is faith a part of everything in my life? It is the moving factor in my life. I've said very often that life is a tenderizing process and a series of lessons in humility; so perhaps when we come back again to our most vulnerable selves in our old age, we will actually come to know the truth of that saying that there is strength in weakness. And faith leads you there. Faith takes you beyond. That's what it means to me.

Wright

When I consider the help we get from each other, the information we get from each other, and the confidence we receive from each other, I'm reminded of one of your friends, Bob Hope. I read a beautiful story you wrote about Mr. Hope that I would like for you to share with our readers. Would you do that?

Jillian

Oh, I would love to share it. It'll be paraphrased from the actual writing, of course, because I don't remember the exact words. The moment that I'm speaking of is 1983. I had always felt, as a child, that one was never really officially a part of this thing called show business until one was asked by Bob Hope and the USO to perform for our peacekeeping troops or our troops who were actually in action. My turn came in 1983, when the hot spot was just off the shores of Beirut, Lebanon. I was asked to come and perform with the USO and Bob for the Sixth Fleet during Christmas time and visit each and every one of the ships with him.

So there he was. It was one of the evenings when we were going back to what we affectionately referred to as the "Beirut Hilton," which was actually the USS Guam anchored off shore. We had just done a performance on one of the other ships, and the director decided he wanted to get a sunset shot that evening, with me singing *Silent Night* with the sunset behind me and the rest of us there. But since it was now curfew, we had to go back on a Foxfire boat instead of a plane. There were boxes of ammunition there. Bob sat down, and all of us were "shaking in our boots," because we had no idea what was about to come up. It was dark. We were on an unfamiliar ocean. I understand there were some pretty nasty things in that ocean. The Navy Seals were saying, "If we capsize, do not call out. We'll find you." And even the idea that these wonderful men would save us didn't help me much.

But then I looked at Bob when we started to go into the ocean, and the wake of the ocean was behind him. There was this eerie kind of a red, low-cast light that was illuminating him, and he was sleeping. Our "old man of the sea" was sleeping and taking it all in stride. I thought to myself, "I am so lucky and so privileged to be here with him." Because I knew that he was charmed, I was going to stay with him. In the sheer darkness, and while our armies were shaking, he was deeply and rhythmically breathing and sleeping and taking all of those naps that he took so well.

He woke up when we started to slow down, and out of nowhere, this immense structure—a very surrealistic sight, the side of this metal monster, the USS Guam—was lit up. The guys got out and docked the Foxfire boat to a platform dock. We were supposed to jump onto that. Well, I took a look at Bob and thought, "You've got to be kidding! If you jump onto that platform and you miss the timing, you're going to get smashed!"

Bob was having his feet massaged to get him going. He got up and he was our fearless leader. He went forward and without missing a beat, he jumped. He was in his eighties at the time. So I looked at my husband, and we were duly embarrassed and ashamed of what we had been thinking, so we took the jump.

The next thing we saw was a rope and metal ladder that fell down several stories along the side of ship, and I said, "No! You've got to be kidding me! We're going to go up this?" So they attached it, and sure enough, Bob started going up. Our pied piper started going up there. And one guy said, "Just don't look down." Well, my palms were sweating. I hate going up ladders. Of course, the first thing you do after someone gives you an instruction is do exactly what they just told you *not* to do. I looked down, and I found out why. I immediately froze to the ladder. I looked up and I saw Bob going up very calmly and over onto the deck of the ship. I thought, "Okay, I can't stop here. I've got to keep going." So I kept looking up, and I thought, "If he can do it, I can do it. If he can do it, I can do it." I got up there, and I got onto the USS Guam.

I remember when we were performing on stage there. At one time in our history, I remember there was a controversy as to whether or not this was a publicity thing that Bob did for himself or something that he had his heart in. I must tell you without a doubt that his heart was in it. Oh, I saw it many times. I would be in the wings, watching him.

I remember one time specifically. Bob must have felt that somebody's eyes were on him. There he was, in the light, watching the people watching Vic Damone singing, and then he sensed it. He turned and he caught me looking at him. He smiled, and his eyes were full of tears. He said, "They're my guys and gals," with such love and such devotion. I could see there were volumes spoken in what he told me. What his face told me was that he considered it a privilege to be there to perform for them. He considered it a privilege to bring laughter to our sons and daughters and sisters and brothers and fathers and mothers who had come upon humorless times, at a time when a little bit of home was the one thing that they wanted for Christmas.

Wright

Right!

Jillian

He brought it there to them and did so for many years, long before I came on the scene. That was the last time he officially went out—that trip during Operation Desert Shield. That was the last time, and

I was privileged enough to witness that. So Bob gave a lot of people a lot of memories. He knew what his position would do for them, but he also introduced them into an area of life that he felt the privilege of feeling.

He introduced all of us to the things that satisfied him on the inside, and he said, "See here. This is what it's all about. This is what is reaching out to those who want a sense of family right now." He was a great patriot, as we all know. He came from England to this country, and this adopted country gave him a beautiful, beautiful future.

Our country is the most wonderful, fabulous country, filled with wonderful, fabulous people, especially those who are willing to go out and uphold the precepts of our country and fight for it and fight for what we believe in—freedom. He wanted to give back to that, because he knew what this country meant to him and what this country gave to him and made possible for him.

Wright
It was a great tribute.

Jillian
You know, I think that he's up there in the arms of our Savior, who is saying, "Well done, my good and faithful servant." It was a privilege to be with him, and I thank him for giving us the memories, and for inviting my family to the shows. My mother and father were invited up to Bob's home in Palm Desert, and my father was introduced to and took pictures with the Blue Angels and so forth, so it was a thrill for him and my mother to see all this.

My son now has the ability to take a look at the memories I have. Bob's wife, Dolores, always loved the picture of me on the cover of one of the magazines—I think it was *Good Housekeeping*, or maybe it was *Ladies Home Journal*. But anyway, I was holding Andy when he was just an infant, and Dolores asked to put it up with her collection of the Madonnas in her home. I was so thrilled with that. You know, I have a frame that was inscribed by them for my son; so my son will also have something to talk about with his children. Bob left a legacy for a lot of people, and he will be grievously missed. I loved him and Dolores dearly.

Wright
I know that you are changing peoples' lives as you go about the country presenting your topics: "I Never Had a Bad Day in My Life,"

"Surviving and Thriving," and "The Winner in You." I know how re-warding that must be, but has talking to and helping people changed you in any way?

Jillian

Talking to other people, I believe, is always a good thing. When I go out, I may talk, but I also have a question-and-answer period. That question-and-answer period runs the gamut. I mean, they ask me about being a mother. They ask me about my medical history. I also get people who come up and tell their stories. They tell of their strug-gles and their triumphs. When we go out there and talk, my energy is totally drained out of me; but I get reenergized by the inspiration I get from the stories of others. So I think it's a cycle. I think it's a cir-cle of breathing out and breathing in—breathing out the information and hopefully, the inspiration and entertainment, and then breathing in the reenergizing and refueling from other people. It's other-oriented, and that's always energizing.

Wright

What a great conversation on faith. We've been talking today with actress, entertainer, and speaker Ann Jillian. Ann, I really appreciate the time you've taken with me today. I know how busy you must be. This has really been enlightening for me, and I am sure it will be for our readers as well. Thank you so much for being with us today on *Speaking of Faith*.

Jillian

It's been a pleasure talking with you, David. Thank you very much.

About The Author

ANN JILLIAN is a three-time Emmy and Golden Globe Award winning actress and singer. Since 1985, she has added motivational speaker to her impressive list of credits, addressing business, medical, professional and women's groups with her own unique blend of humor and inspiration. Ann's programs are fun, informative, and flexible to the clients needs.

Good Housekeeping Magazine named her one of the most admired women of the world. Her prowess extends from the worlds concert halls, to feature film and the Broadway stage. She has starred in over twenty-five television movies, and hundreds of other television appearances. Her television movie, *The Ann Jillian Story* which recounted her victory over breast cancer was the number one film of the television season, but more importantly, it delivered Ann's message about the hopeful side of breast cancer to its millions of viewers. With the birth of her son after cancer, she now adds the title "Working Mom" to her impressive accomplishments. In addition, she is the President of her own production company, 9-J.

Ann Jillian
Andy Murcia, Manager
Phone: 818.501.0807
Fax: 818.501.1887
PO Box 57739
Sherman Oaks, CA. 91413
www.annjillian.com

Chapter 9

NITA SCOGGAN

David Wright (Wright)

Today we're talking with Nita Scoggan. Nita has had an amazing ministry for twenty-five years in Washington, D.C. She has written seventeen books, been interviewed on many television programs, and has been a keynote speaker at hundreds of events across the nation. If that were not enough, in 1984 she was invited to hold weekly prayer services for staffers at the White House each week. She did this throughout three Presidential Administrations: Reagan, Bush, and Clinton, until December 1998.

Nita, welcome to *Conversations on Faith*.

How did this happen? What kind of strings did you pull to get invited to such an honored position?

Nita Scoggan (Scoggan)

David, it is truly amazing, because I didn't have any strings to pull. I was a government employee working in the basement of the Pentagon. I had been teaching daily lunchtime Bible classes for professional women on staff for over ten years. My ministry was credentialed through the Armed Forces Chaplaincy Board. God was answering prayers and many miracles were happening in the meetings, but I doubted that anybody had ever heard about me or what God had been doing for women who gave their lunch hour to God. It has been no surprise when folks have asked me how I was chosen for this important position.

Frankly, it wasn't something I had planned, hoped for, or dreamed about doing. It just never entered my mind that I would ever be involved in ministry at the White House, where the most vital decisions affecting the nation are made!

But, I was faithful in the workplace ministry God had given me to do.

As I said, I never thought about great things, I just told the Lord I would do whatever He wanted me to do, and go where He wanted me to go. But I did pray that God would always have my husband, Bill, go with me. We were a team and had been married almost thirty years at that time.

Well, this is what happened: In 1984, we attended a weekend prayer conference in D.C., with well-known men in ministry such as Charles Stanley and Bill Bright. One woman, Carolyn Sundseth, the Associate Director of Public Affairs on President Ronald Reagan's staff, brought a greeting from the President and did a great job representing him. After the program ended, I thanked Carolyn her for representing Christian women nationwide as well as the President.

Carolyn asked, "Nita, could you wait a few minutes until I greet the others in line? I want to talk to you for a minute."

"Oh, sure," I replied, and stepped aside. A few minutes later we talked.

Carolyn said, "I want to start a weekly Bible study and prayer service in my office while I am at the White House."

"That's a great idea," I said. "It has been such a blessing for women in pressure-cooker jobs at the Pentagon."

"I want to have a dynamite class like yours at the Pentagon," she said. "I've heard of the amazing answers to prayers and even miracles happening at lunchtime."

I was surprised she had heard of my ministry, but God was definitely blessing us in powerful, dynamic ways.

Carolyn said she had many friends in ministry all over the nation who wanted to move to Washington, D.C., in order to conduct the meetings in her office at lunchtime. In spite of this, Carolyn told them, "This ministry isn't mine to give. It is God's class and He will choose the person to lead it."

Then, Carolyn pointed her finger at me and said, "And, Nita, *you're* the one God has chosen."

Wright

How did you feel when Carolyn said that *you* were God's choice for the White House?

Scoggan

I was overwhelmed and surprised. My mouth probably fell open. I was thrilled, yet humbled. As a working wife and mother for most of my life, I was afraid I wouldn't fit in or be respected as a Bible teacher and prayer leader by important people on the White House staff.

"It's such an honor to be asked, Carolyn," I said. "I'd love to do it, but I'll have to ask my husband. I'm pretty busy and he may not want me to add anything else. So, I'll ask him and call you in the morning."

On the way home, I told Bill what Carolyn had said. I told Bill that I felt unworthy and was probably too busy to accept.

Bill said, "You told God you'd go wherever He wanted you to go. Are you going to say no now to a door He has opened for you?"

"If you want me to, I won't say no," I replied. "But it's a big commitment, honey," I reminded him. "It will take most of my day, commuting into Washington, finding parking, getting cleared into the White House, etc. It's definitely missionary work; there is no pay or compensation, just like the Pentagon. Carolyn told me there aren't enough parking permits for the staff, 'so don't expect to get help with parking.' Ministry is a walk of faith."

I claimed the scripture 1 Thess. 5:24 which says that God, who had called me, would be faithful and enable me to do it. I felt confident in His promise.

As we climbed into bed that night, I said, "My motto should be 'Have Bible will travel—anywhere He leads I'll go.' "

The next day, I telephoned the White House and told Carolyn I could do it. A few days later, we held our first meeting in her office. It was great, but I could see my schedule had to change.

I was still teaching classes at the Pentagon. About fifty women gave their lunchtime to come each day to pray and study the Bible. This meeting had started small with seven women and then grew to standing room only. When all the chairs were filled, women sat on the floor and latecomers stood around the room. Why? God really blessed us because we believed His Word, acted on the Word, and sacrificed our lunch to put Him first in our life.

Lunchtime at the Pentagon was exciting! God answered lots of prayers as marriages were saved, children's lives were changed and protected, and many women were prayed for and healed. It was God's power! Our lunchtime was truly a "power lunch"!

Bill and I decided that my ministry at the Pentagon would have to change, from teaching daily to teaching once a week, and I had to do it immediately.

Wright

That is interesting—after ten years of daily ministry you were able to suddenly change to only teaching once a week. Wasn't it difficult to find women to take on a big commitment to teach your daily classes?

Scoggan

It could have been terrible, but God had worked this out, too.

This is what happened: Years prior to this time, I had felt God saying that I was doing too much, teaching classes five days a week. He impressed me that I was a poor leader! *A poor leader?* That really hurt me! Everyone said I was doing a great job—teaching, praying, and providing biblical counseling for women from many different denominations. But, God explained that I was a poor leader because I didn't train other women to do the work of the ministry. So, the next day I told the women I was starting a leadership training program.

Over the years, I had chosen six faithful women, knowledgeable in God's Word, to serve as "Council Ring leaders" over the women's ministry. These were my leaders. I trained them in many leadership skills and how to handle problems. Of course, they had seen how I managed various situations throughout the years, so they had learned "on the job." Then, I gave them opportunities to teach the Bible and lead prayer sessions. In that way I had gradually cut down on the days of the week I taught.

When I announced my invitation to teach at the White House and that I could only teach once a week at the Pentagon, these great women in leadership were equipped—"armed and ready"—to step up and lead.

Wright

Tell us about your ministry at the White House. Was it the same as what you had done at the Pentagon?

Scoggan

I thought it would be, but I was in for a surprise. God had something new in store for me. At the White House we met in Carolyn's office, which was just a few steps away from the Vice President's office. I thought it would be a ministry to women. But men, as well as women, came to the first two meetings. The first time, I told the men they couldn't stay because it was a ladies' meeting. But they said, "Well, this is Carolyn's office and she invited us!"

So, I said, "Well then, I guess you can stay."

But, I didn't feel comfortable with men in the class. I didn't want to teach or take authority over them. I had turned down a number of promotions at the Pentagon because I didn't believe God wanted me to supervise men. Not everyone agreed with me on that, but it is a scriptural principle. Some people told me not to worry—just teach the women as I always do; if the men want to come and listen, okay—don't worry.

I asked Bill to pray with me that God would open a meeting for the men. Early in the morning of the third week, I was praying about the situation and it was like a light turned on in my brain. God spoke to my heart, "Invite Bill to join you to teach and lead the class."

After breakfast I asked Bill to come with me and help lead the class. He said, "No way! I'm too busy. I don't want to be with all women. You were the one invited to teach—it's *your* ministry!"

As his helpmate, I felt that I should help Bill "see the light."

"But honey," I urged, "we could be like Priscilla and Acquilla. We can be team-teachers and teach the Word more perfectly. I'll feel better and I'm sure the men *and* the women will feel good having a team there. Please, honey," I begged, "if you'll just go with me this one time and you don't like it, I won't ask you anymore."

"Okay," Bill replied. "But if no men attend, I'm not going back."

"Lord, you heard that," I said, as I looked up toward heaven. "If you want Bill and me to be a team, please let those men come to the class today."

That day, the White House had been closed to visitors due to a bomb threat. We weren't sure we would be allowed in, but we were cleared. The meeting room had been changed, so we walked along an unfamiliar corridor looking for the assigned room. Suddenly, a door opened and a man walked out and came over to us.

"Step back against the wall," he said. We backed up to the wall and he moved close to us, with his hand up about chest high. We had our Visitor Badges on and I thought maybe he was going to search us, but he didn't. We just stood there, wondering what was going on, when the door opened again and out walked President Reagan, smiling and followed by a large contingent of the press. In the narrow hallway we were close enough to shake his hand. "It's the President!" I thought; but I was so astonished I don't think I even breathed. I'll never forget the thrill of it. It was as though we were frozen in space. I didn't even say, "God bless you!" I didn't say anything; neither did Bill. We just stood there watching him as he walked away, smiling and talking to his aides.

After the President left the area, the man put his hand down and told us we could go. We asked directions to a certain room and as it turned out, the room to which we were assigned was the room where the President had just held a press conference. What a place to meet and pray for our leaders!

When the staffers gathered for the class, several of the men were there. Bill was heartily welcomed and he enjoyed every minute. Our team ministry began. We told the class about our experience seeing the President so close and personal. Several people said they had worked there for years and had never seen the President in person. I felt it was a special blessing God had planned for Bill, and for me too.

From that day on, Bill and I were team teachers. We didn't even have time to read a book on *how* to do it—God just enabled us to be effective.

Wright

Did you feel any special calling when God chose you and Bill as team teachers at the White House? Where did you meet?

Scoggan

I am sure we were chosen to speak and teach words of faith and to encourage prayer among the staff because of the perilous times in which we are living. We had the honor of leading meetings at the White House Executive Offices for nearly fifteen years. We met in Carolyn Sundseth's office until she retired. After George W. Bush became President, we were assigned Room 180 for weekly meetings. It is a very special conference room located near the Oval Office. It had been Vice President George Bush's office! A plaque outside that room states: "This room was the Vice President's office from Herbert Hoover to George W. Bush."

I thought, "What a wonderful place to pray!" The Vice President's office was almost directly above our conference room, so we were able to see Vice Presidents from the various administrations quite often, coming or going, in the hallways, or on the stairs.

Bill and I would arrive early at the White House to pray. As we walked the halls we asked for Godly wisdom for the staff and directors of each office.

It never ceased to amaze me that God had chosen to take me to the White House for such a time as this in America. I was chosen for God's purpose! I believe that purpose was, and still is, to pray for all in authority, pray for God's mercy on America, pray for America to turn back to the Bible and to the morals that made our country great. Prayer was the first thing we did.

God impressed me to pray for our key historic or government buildings. We did this, knowing that prayer avails much. The White House holds a special place in our history. I believe God placed me there to pray for His protection over this vital building.

Wright

Can you share with us any specific answer to the prayers you prayed for the White House or other historic buildings?

Scoggan

Yes, I sure can! I remember one day the class prayed *twice* for God's protection over the White House and First Family. The very next day, we heard the early morning news report of a small airplane crashing into the White House during the dark of night.

Later that day, we learned that it was a private rental plane and the pilot had been killed on impact. It had been no accident. The pilot had turned off all his lights, flew low to avoid radar, crossed restricted air space around Washington, and headed straight for the White House before he was spotted. It was too late for anyone to prevent the attack. Evidently, the target was the Presidential living quarters, but a wing struck a huge Magnolia tree and the plane crashed to the ground just outside the Oval Office! It was nothing short of a miracle. It was later publicized as a "pilot error." When we get to heaven perhaps we'll see a re-play, like those done on television during sports events, and we'll discover how many attacks were averted and lives were saved because we prayed.

When I led women's classes at the Pentagon (from 1973 to 1993), we prayed for angels to walk the halls and protect the people and the building. There were many times we received bomb threats and our offices were notified to look for suspicious packages or unusual items left in our work areas. Again, prayer availed much and either the bombs didn't go off or they were found and disarmed. Truly there were many miracles. Those prayers were based on our faith in God's promises:

❏ *"No weapon formed against you shall prosper . . ."*—Isaiah 54:17.

❏ *"Call unto me and I will answer thee and show thee great and mighty things . . ."*— Jeremiah 33:3.

Wright

Nita, do you have a message regarding prayer that you are passionate about?

Scoggan

Yes, David, I do. *I want to encourage all of our readers to become active prayer warriors.* Much depends on whether we will actually pray, not just talk about prayer! We *are* in a real war; it is a spiritual battle as well. Muslim nations hate America because we are seen as a "Christian" nation. They declared a "holy war"—a *jihad*—on America back in the 1970s. Somehow, it wasn't taken seriously by most citizens.

In November 1979 Iran attacked our embassy and took sixty-six American citizens captive, many of them were held hostage for over a year! Eight servicemen from the all-volunteer Joint Special Operations Group were killed in an aborted attempt to rescue the hostages. On October 23, 1983, a Marine barracks compound in Beirut, Lebanon, was bombed and 241 people were killed.

I can tell you that America's military leaders took this war seriously, while many in Congress chose to cut the defense budget again and again. It broke my heart to see that our military was forced to divert funds, originally appropriated for training, and spare parts to send to our troops in order to provide United Nations peacekeeping.

While our military was being stretched thin protecting other countries, many bases were being closed! It was insane then and the insanity continues with more bases closed and defense budgets cut. Naval facilities such as the Long Beach Naval Base in California, classified in 1990s as "no longer needed," was leased to the China Ocean Shipping Company (COSCO) for ninety-nine years under the Clinton Administration. COSCO is an arm of the Communist Chinese government. My book, *Prayer Alert: It's Now or Never*, covers this and many important issues you don't usually find in the nightly news that are vital key items for our prayers (available on my Web site www.NitaScoggan.com).

If you love America and enjoy its freedoms, I'm calling you to pray daily and:

1. Join a prayer group.
2. Help observe the annual National Day of Prayer (NDP) on every first Thursday in May by holding a patriotic event to pray for America in your community. My husband and I are NDP County Coordinators, organizing civic groups, churches, government, and military leaders to gather and join millions nationwide for NDP events of thanksgiving and prayers.
3. Join the http://www.governorsprayerteam.com/ and pray for your own state.

In January 2006, we were asked to head a prayer organization for the state of Indiana, the "Governor's Prayer Team." Rev. Tom Walker birthed the vision for citizens praying for their Governor and leaders in Indiana in 2005. The idea spread quickly and governors from other states asked for a similar prayer organization. Rev. Walker organized a national Board of Directors and began recruiting state prayer leaders who in turn will recruit prayer leaders in big cities and rural areas. It's a huge task, with no funding.

We're all so busy and I'm no different. I started to say "No" to Tom. But, then I thought, "If I won't give my time to pray, who will?" I know the need is great at such a time as this so I said, "Yes!"

The Bible shows God's desire for intercessors to pray. In Ezekiel 22:30, we read that God said, *"I sought for a man among them, that should make up the hedge, and stand in the gap before me for the land, that I should not destroy it: but I found none."* In Ezekiel's day, scripture says that God was searching for a prayer warrior but *"found none."*

God uses ordinary people like you and me. He's waiting for us to pray. Will *you* say, "Yes, I'll pray for God's mercy on America and not to destroy our land"?

Wright

Nita, after years of ministry, will you share some ideas or keys to help people to become more effective in ministry?

Scoggan

Yes, David, I sure will. I've found there are five keys to being effective in ministry:

1. **We must have total faith that God's Word applies to us today**. Hebrews 11:6 says, *"But without faith it is impossible to please him: for he that cometh to God must believe that he is, and that he is a rewarder of them that diligently seek him."* It is absolutely vital that we believe God's Word is true, and that it applies to us today. In Mark 11:22 Jesus said, *"Have faith in God."* We must believe that God can and *will* do, for us what the Bible says He will do.

2. **We must pray**. Mark 11:24 says, *"What things soever ye desire, when ye pray, believe that ye receive them, and ye shall have them."* It takes faith to believe that you already *have* received things you need, *when* you pray. Anyone can believe they receive what they asked for *when* they see it. However, faith believes God, that you have already received before you see it, you just know you will see it soon.

3. **We must ask in faith, claim God's promises, without doubting**. James 1:6, 7 warns, *"But let him ask in faith, nothing wavering. For he that wavereth . . . let not that man think he shall receive any thing of the Lord."* If God says it, we must believe it or we can't expect to receive anything from Him.

4. **We must act on the Word**. James 1:22 says, *"Be ye doers of the Word, and not hearers only . . ."* Keith Moore, founder and president of Moore Life Ministries and Faith Life Church in Branson, Missouri, sings of the importance of acting on God's Word in a song from his album *Healing in His Wings*, titled "God's Got a Miracle For You." A small excerpt inspires me,

"Act on the Word, act like it's true . . . just step up and step out, do what you could not do. Act on the Word, act like it's true."

5. **We must be listening for God's guidance**. Acts 9:11 gives an ex-ample of this, *"And the Lord said unto him, Arise, and go into the street which is called Straight, and inquire . . . for one called Saul, of Tarsus: for, behold, he prayeth . . ."* It's so important to be open and listening for God's voice. He knows those who pray fervent prayers and who will intercede in times of an urgent crisis.

Let me share an example, of being led to pray when you don't know specifically *what* or *whom* you are praying for.

One day, when my Pentagon class had concluded and most of the women had left to return to their offices, God said to me, "Pray for President Reagan."

I was picking up my Bible and stopped in mid-air. "But, Lord," I said, "We've already prayed for the President."

"Pray now," was God's response.

"Ladies," I called loudly, "could some of you stay for a minute? I believe God wants us to pray an urgent prayer for President Reagan."

Five women joined hands with me for a quick, fervent prayer for the protection of the President and that God would meet every need.

Then, we hurriedly returned to our workplaces. Minutes later, in my office, the radio announced that President Reagan had been shot! There were almost no details at that moment except that he was shot on the street outside the downtown Hilton Hotel, where he had given a speech, and was rushed to the hospital.

The next few days brought much more information about the at-tempt to kill the President. Doctors were not sure he would live—the bullet was only a fraction of an inch from his heart. But, he lived!

We rejoiced that God had called us to pray, almost at the instant of the attack! God was merciful and our prayers availed much.

Many people may have been praying as well as our group, but I know the prayers of women at the Pentagon availed much, and touched the heart of God.

Wright

You have written seventeen books, many of them deal with prayer. Are there thoughts you'd like to share about the importance of prayer for America?

Scoggan

Yes, David. I've spoken around the nation on dangerous issues facing America. I want to shout *America, wake up!* (That is the title of one of my first books.) Working in the Pentagon made me very aware of the goals of Communism for world domination and those goals have never changed. Perestroika, and the "fall" of communism, was an attempt to deceive the West, and with talks of peace, lull people into believing that Russia was no longer an enemy.

My book, *It's Now or Never: Prayer Alert,* deals with active Communism in America and around the world—especially in Cuba and Central America. Many fighters have been trained to hate America and there are plans to cross into our borders and kill Americans.

There is plenty of documentation; unfortunately, many people just don't want to hear "bad news." They prefer to watch *Wheel of Fortune* or some fun entertainment and ignore anything "negative." They listen to speakers who speak "good news" saying that peace and prosperity are in store for Christians in America.

But, God's Word points to judgment for wickedness and America has scoffed at sin and legislated immorality. Our repentance and prayers for God's mercy and forgiveness are vital!

We must be informed if we are to pray effectively. If people don't know what's happening, they won't know what to pray about. This must read book, *It's Now or Never: Prayer Alert* (available at www.NitaScoggan.com) reveals a lot about the dangers facing America because of Red China's military buildup. People are shocked to learn that America has allowed an arm of the Chinese Communist government—China Ocean Shipping Company (COSCO)—to take over the strategic but "no longer needed" Long Beach Naval Base in California.

Col. Jim Ammerman, U.S. Army (Ret.), provided a photo of one warehouse with the full COSCO name prominently displayed on the building, behind a high fence with barbed wire. Col. Ammerman reported talking to local police and U.S. Customs inspectors who said, "Only a slim sampling of cargo was inspected. Already contraband automatic weapons and ammo were found to be entering. Most favored nation (MFN), you know."—*CFGC, July 1999, p. 45.*

Hutchison Whampoa, Limited, a front company for Communist China, now has operational control of both ends of the Panama Canal. The U.S. turned over the Panama Canal to Panama on December 31, 1999. According to military experts, China poses another threat by establishing a new base in the Bahamas only sixty miles from the United States.

It's heartbreaking to find there are great multitudes who only want to hear about prosperity and good news. Many churches aim to make their people happy. God is calling for prayer and repentance; but they focus on keeping their congregations entertained.

We can't depend on the secular media to keep us informed. I'm still a research analyst at heart—I read and study a lot—and my conclusion is "what you don't know *can* hurt you." So, I write and speak out at every opportunity to warn Americans of growing dangers.

I often feel like Queen Esther, exposing evil. She came from a humble beginning—a woman of no important background—but God chose her to be a queen in the kingdom of Ahasuerus—a kingdom that reached from India to Ethiopia. God brought Esther to the king's palace to stand in the gap for her nation. David, do you remember the evil scheme planned for the entire Jewish nation? All Hebrew men, women, and children were to be killed in one day! Esther was willing to stand up and speak up, but she prayed and fasted first. She then spoke up and exposed the person behind the evil plan. Her faith and courage turned the situation around and saved the nation.

Years ago, in the Pentagon, I often felt like crying for America and our military people. I am still thankful for the blessing of just being an American and living in the freest nation in the world. With all its faults, it's a grand nation—my home sweet home. I am still urging people to pray, repent of our nation's sins, and stand in the gap pleading for God's mercy, that He will not to destroy our land. Remember Ezekiel 22:30: *"I sought for a man among them, that should make up the hedge, and stand in the gap before me* for the land, that I should not destroy it, *but I found none."* It is shocking! With God's judgment hanging over the nation, there was not one intercessor! People may have been praying for health, finances, or their family, but no one was praying for God's mercy to spare their land!

Wright

You've given over 2,000 speeches across the nation. You are a member of the National Speakers Association and the International

Speakers Network. Can you share some keys you've used for success in preparing these messages?

Scoggan

I believe there are three key things that are vital:

1. *To pray and seek God's guidance* because each meeting is different. Even though I may be speaking for a chapter that is part of a national organization, the needs for each group may be slightly different. For example, I've been invited to be the speaker for Concerned Women for America at National or State Conventions, and other programs in Maryland, Indiana, D.C., Virginia, California and Alaska. The topic or focus of each message is very unique. I can't use a frequently used "canned" message if I want to be effective.

2. *To fast.* Even if I can only give up one meal, it is a powerful spiritual aid. God calls fasting a sacrifice in which you afflict your soul, giving up something you really like. Don't give up eating pork rinds or snails if you dislike them anyway; that doesn't count. Give up favorite foods—then it's a sacrifice.

3. *To spend time studying scriptures that apply to the topic.* Even if I don't use them in my message, it gives me powerful authority in speaking.

Wright

I was fascinated when you mentioned a "canned" message. Will you share with us a time when you planned your speech and changed it at the last minute?

Scoggan

I sure will! It's happened a number of times, but one incident really impressed me about the importance of hearing from God and being led by the Holy Spirit.

An unusual thing occurred, one I won't forget, when I was invited to speak at a Christian women's luncheon in a southern state. My husband, Bill, and I arrived the day before the meeting, having been invited to stay in the home of Joanne, the President of the organization. As we three sat down to dinner, her attractive teenage daughter hurried in and joined us. During the meal I invited her to come to the luncheon, but she had other things to do and declined. After dinner, the girl said goodnight and went up to her room.

Joanne and I got better acquainted as we talked while I washed the dishes and she put things away. Joanne explained that her husband worked in another city and only got home on weekends. "So, it's very nice to have company," she said.

I couldn't help but notice a "kitchen witch"—the cute kind of cloth doll dressed in gingham, with a peaked black hat, riding on a broom—hanging above the sink. Since the Bible mentions witches in negative terms, I wondered why a Christian woman would have that in her home. But, I kept quiet.

Joanne shared that they had been struggling with many health problems and bills. She didn't understand why God would let them have financial problems. I suggested we pray together about a breakthrough. As she talked I couldn't forget about the witch over the sink, so I asked her where she got the "kitchen witch."

"What witch?" Joanne asked. I indicated the one that was hanging above her kitchen sink. She got up, took it down and looked at it. "I never knew what it was! I just thought it was cute and hung it up. It was a gift from a friend at work," Joanne said.

I suggested that it might be having a negative influence in their lives.

"I'll throw this out right now!" Joanne exclaimed.

"Wait!" I said. "This should be burned if possible, so no one else picks it up and takes it to their house."

"We can burn it in the fireplace when my husband gets home," she said.

"Meanwhile, why don't you cut it up into small pieces," I suggested, "and just put it in the fireplace until he gets home." So, she did it then and there.

We were tired and turned in early. Joanne said, "I'll call you about 5:30. I've got things all ready to fix a nice breakfast." We said our goodnights and went downstairs to the basement guest room.

In the wee hours, I awakened feeling like someone was choking me. I tried to wake Bill up, but I could only whisper. "Honey, pray for me!" I said. "I feel like someone is choking me!"

Bill prayed, rebuking every spirit and claiming the protection of the blood of Jesus over us. I felt an immediate release and I could breathe again.

"Honey," I asked, "Can you smell that strong smell of incense?"

"No," he replied. (Bill's sinus problems prevented him from smelling. I couldn't expect him to smell it.) Bill rolled over and went back to sleep.

I stayed there in bed praying, wondering what was going on. Then the Lord spoke to me. He wanted me to speak on the dangers of witchcraft and occult involvement at the luncheon.

"Are you sure, Lord?" I asked. "These are all Christian women and they probably already know all about those things."

God was silent.

"Okay, Lord, I'll get up early and prepare."

I awoke before anyone else was up and told Bill I was going to fast because I needed God's blessing on my speech. As I prepared, I prayed and put out a fleece. "Lord," I prayed, "If you really want me to speak on the dangers of the occult, please let Joanne's daughter, Lisa, come to the luncheon." That was a big request—she didn't want to attend, but that wasn't too much for God.

The luncheon was really nice. When I was introduced I looked over the audience, Lisa wasn't there. But, as I opened my Bible, I saw Lisa enter the back of the auditorium.

"Okay, Lord," I prayed silently, "help me say what is on your heart for these women."

Later, after concluding my message, I offered to pray only for those who had been involved in the occult or witchcraft—if anyone wanted prayer for other needs, the organization's officers would pray with them. No one came forward. I waited and waited. Finally, a very pretty young woman came forward. I whispered, "You must not have understood. I am only praying for those who were in the occult."

She said, "I have been a witch." I could hardly believe it—she was so pretty and young—not the stereotypical ugly woman with a mole on her nose like ones I'd seen in the movies.

"Well, honey," I said, "Jesus came to set you free from that, but you need to renounce all the works of darkness you've been involved in and pray with me to receive Jesus Christ as your Savior."

"I need to tell you something else," she said. "I was also a vampire."

I was shocked. I had never seen a vampire, except in movies and their teeth were like long fangs. She was shorter than I was, so I stooped down and asked to see her teeth. No fangs. Her teeth looked normal to me.

"Did you ever drink blood?" I asked.

"Oh, yes," she replied. "That was required."

"Well, honey," I said, "None of that is too much for the Lord Jesus. He can set you free from being in bondage to all of this wicked activity. First of all, you need to pray and ask Jesus to be your Savior."

"I don't know how to pray or what to say," she told me.

"Okay, bow your head and repeat this after me," I said. "Lord Jesus, I ask you to be my Lord and Savior."

She started to pray, "Lord Je—" She tried to say it again, "Lord Je—" The third time she tried to say "Jesus," but when she said "Lord Jes—" suddenly, the evil spirit in her hurled her down violently. She landed several feet away from me and crashed into a chair that hit the wall. I heard a loud crack! The girl lay motionless on the floor. I rushed over and knelt down beside her and started to pray. The president came over to join me in prayer and she knelt beside the young woman.

"Oh, dear God," I prayed, "don't let her die!"

Then I began to take authority over the demonic forces. "In the name of Jesus," I said, "I command all of these tormenting spirits to come out of her, right now, in Jesus' name!"

The president was on the floor beside me praying too.

Then, the girl opened her eyes and sat up. We helped her stand and she said, "I felt a great weight lifted from me."

I asked her to come back to the platform and we would pray the prayer that could change her life forever. She did. This time, she had no problem repenting, praying to receive Jesus as her Lord and Savior, and renouncing all the occult activity she had been involved in. She looked like a different person—so happy and bright. She thanked me and thanked me for being persistent in prayer for her.

After this, four more women came to me for deliverance from spirits of the occult that had entered their lives as a result of their occult involvement.

David, you can see why I said that it is absolutely necessary to be prayed up, filled with the knowledge of God's Word every day, and fast regularly. We just don't know what kinds of spiritual needs there are that we may have to face in our ministry to people.

Wright

Was it always easy for you to stand on God's promises, or did you ever have a real challenge to hold onto your faith?

Scoggan

Yes, David, I sure faced a real spiritual battle in 1998 when my husband, Bill, became very sick. Doctors thought he was having mini-strokes, but said there was no cure. Tests couldn't find anything wrong; but something *was* dreadfully wrong. Bill had occasional unresponsive moments when he couldn't talk, which greatly frightened me. He didn't feel good and wanted to stay in bed. Not only that but he was also suffering memory loss. God was my only help because the doctors couldn't help me.

I prayed for wisdom and felt God was saying we needed to move and be near Bill's family in rural Indiana. Bill brightened right up when I suggested it. We prayed God would provide someone with a shepherd's heart to take over our White House ministry and we asked the class members to pray too.

We put our house up for sale and flew to Indiana for a weekend to house-hunt. We searched, but left disappointed. Two weeks later, the realtor called and the very house we wanted had just been listed again. "Hold it," we said, and flew back to Indiana. We walked through the house, and bought it. Our Virginia home sold quickly, but the buyers couldn't move in until January 4, which gave us time to pack.

We had worked in Washington, D.C. for forty years and had been blessed with family and many great friends there. Active as teachers in a big church, besides our ongoing ministry at the White House and Pentagon for nearly twenty-five years, moving from Washington wasn't in our retirement plans. However, Bill's health mattered more than anything. I kept packing day after day.

It was like a whirlwind. On our two trips to Indiana, a highly recommended pastor—a man of prayer—filled in for us. The pastor said he really had a heart for the people working at the White House, so we felt this was the answer for which we had prayed.

A beautiful farewell luncheon was held for us in mid-December in the Indian Treaty Room of the White House, a very historic room and the scene of many important events. It was one of my favorite rooms because there are life-sized statues of angels in each corner of the room. We were very blessed as our oldest son, Lew, his wife Kay, and several dear ministry friends flew in to help celebrate the occasion. We received a letter from President Clinton commending our years of ministry to the staff and a magnificent plaque of the three Presidents, Reagan, Bush and Clinton, under whose administrations we had ministered as chaplains. What a happy time it was—until class members lined up to say thanks for our ministry; my tears flowed.

In those nearly fifteen years of ministry to the White House staff, lives had changed for eternity. With Christ as Savior, many were healed physically through prayer. We saw many answers to prayer. As hard as it was to say goodbye, we were happy knowing the ministry there would continue.

The moving van arrived and our belongings had to be loaded in the snow. It was after 9 p.m. on January 3, 1999, as we left Virginia for our new life in Indiana.

I was totally depending on the Lord to heal Bill and help me care for him because he was going downhill fast. I was leaving my family, friends, and ministry behind, facing an uncertain future in Indiana—a place I had only visited. Not knowing anyone except Bill's brothers and sisters, I prayed God would help me to be happy. I didn't want to be a bitter woman, always complaining and missing everything left behind. I asked God to restore Bill's memory and health and make me happy in my new home. It was a big request, but nothing is too hard for God.

We quickly made friends and settled in a good Bible-teaching church—the one Bill had attended while growing up. We saw several doctors, all of whom diagnosed Bill with Alzheimer's disease and mini-strokes. They prescribed the only medication available to help with memory loss, but said there was no cure. I kept praying in spite of everyone saying it was hopeless, including an internist, four neurologists, and a psychologist. Bill's health was deteriorating and he could no longer drive. He didn't seem to understand what was going on and couldn't remember our address, or phone number, or what year it was. I was advised to get an attorney and get everything legally in order "while Bill can still write his name!"

David, you asked if I had any really big challenge? This was like a huge mountain of defeat and loss. But I kept praying. Every time Bill asked me to pray when he didn't feel good, I laid hands on him and prayed a prayer of faith. I claimed God's promise that "By Jesus' stripes Bill was healed" (1 Peter 2:24). And I rebuked every symptom tormenting him, commanding them to leave. I remembered that Jesus rebuked the spirit of infirmity and I rebuked that in Bill as well as any other spirit around him.

I had to hold on to God's promises like a bulldog with a bone. Nothing was going to keep me from believing that God was able to heal Alzheimer's. There had to be hope for God's people! I felt God was saying "nutrition."

So, I started reading everything I could find on diet and nutrition, as well as memory loss, dementia, and Alzheimer's disease. I started using everything recommended in the way of vitamins. Bill stayed on a prescription drug for four years, continuing to see the neurologists as well; but he grew worse, not better.

One day, I received an article from a friend who was into nutritional supplements. It was titled "Dementia." Studies using Phosphatydilserine (PS) were very encouraging. Many patients *regained some memory* and ability to care for themselves. I had already tried Gingko and several other memory aids, but could see no improvement in Bill's condition. Reading the article on PS was the first encouragement I'd had. Doctors said he would soon be in a nursing home! So, I had nothing to lose and everything to gain if PS worked. It was expensive, but so was the prescription medication he was taking!

I decided to order a three-month supply of Phosphatydilserine. Bill took 300 milligrams three times a day and I kept praying for a miracle of healing. I could see small changes and ordered another three-month supply of PS. Bill's memory gradually improved. I could see a big difference by six months. I rejoiced and praised the Lord as he remembered what month or year it was, who the president was, or where our cereal bowls were kept. Within that year, Bill could remember lots of things and wanted to get outdoors to help in the yard for the first time in six years. It was a real miracle!

Bill continued to see the neurologist and stayed on the prescription in addition to taking Phosphatydilserine. Two years passed. Bill's abilities recovered, he's allowed to drive, and he's off the prescription drug. His sense of humor has returned and he's enjoying life, doing things that he had forgotten how to do years ago.

I'm taking Phosphatydilserine also. Doctors and nutritionists recommend that anyone over thirty years old should start taking these supplements. Nothing is impossible with God. My advice to readers who need a miracle is: Hold on to your confidence and total faith in the Lord. Believe His promises. Stand on the Word, and let God take it from there.

Wright

Thank you for sharing with us your wonderful stories and events of God's loving care. It was a great encouragement. God bless you.

Scoggan

I am blessed to have the opportunity to tell everyone that we serve a living Savior—our Lord Jesus! Nothing is too hard for Him. He is still in the miracle business!

About The Author

NITA SCOGGAN is a national keynote, seminar, and international conference speaker. She is the award-winning author of seventeen books, professional member of the National Speakers Association, respected Adjunct Professor, and business owner. With enthusiasm and humor she relates success principles learned in her twenty-five-year career as a research analyst and illustrator at the Pentagon. In 2004, Nita was appointed President of the Advisory Board for Oakland City University Bedford (Indiana). As a member of the OCUB faculty, she teaches Business and Liberal Arts courses. A frequent television guest on national and Canadian programs, Nita stresses the value of education in order to be more successful.

From 1973 to 1993, Nita gave her lunchtime to God by teaching daily prayer and Bible classes at the Pentagon. Her ministry is credentialed by the Department of Defense Armed Forces Chaplaincy Board. In 1984, Nita was invited to the White House to conduct weekly ministry to the White House staffers. For almost fifteen years, from Presidents Reagan to Clinton, teaching focused on prayer, believing faith, and being doers of the Word.

Nita Scoggan is a remarkable woman of faith. Born at her grandmother's home, a two-pound preemie at birth, the doctor declared she had "no chance to live." But live she did! Placed in a shoebox, fed with an eyedropper—without medical aid—her survival was a miracle. She overcame health problems and poverty, giving God the credit for it all. "I believe in miracles! I've seen them, in answer to prayer. I know God can do anything, so I love to pray," says Nita. Her driving force is to uplift, encourage, and empower others to achieve their maximum potential in life. Her motto is "Never give up your dreams—pursue them with patience and persistence."

Nita Scoggan

Maximum Zone Consulting

P.O. Box 2125

Bedford, IN 47421-7125

E-mail: nscoggan@ocub.oak.edu

To Schedule Nita to Speak:

www.NitaScoggan.com

Chapter 10

DESIREE CARTER

David E. Wright (Wright)

Today we're talking with Reverend Desiree Carter, pastor, change agent, motivational speaker, teacher, and author. As a speaker she has educated and empowered audiences nationally, providing tools and creating an atmosphere that calls people to commit to their true selves. Her life's journey and experiences have called her to provide self-esteem, life skills, stress relief training, team building, and how to manage conflict, both individuality and corporately. As a motivational speaker she inspires, educates, and empowers others to take risks, choosing growth over fear. Desiree's seminars and workshops challenge her audiences to not be defined by circumstances nor by the choices they make. She says we are not our choices.

Reverend Carter, welcome to *Speaking of Faith!*

Desiree Carter (Carter)

Thank you.

Wright

In your own words, will you describe to our readers what faith means to you?

Carter

When I think about faith, the word "believing" comes to mind—believing in the only power higher than myself: God. Faith calls me to believe and challenges me to walk in "Holy Boldness." Holy Boldness asks me to walk with humanity in spite of them and myself.

Faith is like a delectable chocolate cake, tantalizing my spirit to want to experience more and more of the God who created the universe. Faith causes me to seek intimacy with a God who promises that life does not have to be miserable. Faith gently caresses my soul when life throws its season of winter into my life. The times in life when nothing goes right, when the bills are due and I can't pay them, or when sickness comes upon me and doctors can't help, Faith calls me to stand strong, believing in God's power to not only transform, but to resurrect.

Not even death deters me from the love of God. If someone held a weapon to my head and said, give me your faith in God or die, I would have to die. It has been my faith that has sustained me throughout my life's experiences. It is because of faith that I keep growing and believing in Jesus Christ, the Holy Spirit, and God. It is my faith that calls me to worship and to live a life of love for humanity.

Wright

When you get frustrated, what keeps you on your journey of faith?

Carter

God has instilled love in my heart for humanity. God has given me gifts and skills such as working within the areas of domestic violence, working with youth at risk, and with persons suffering from alcohol and drug abuse. God calls me to use those gifts so that others will know Him and will come to Him. Just as Jesus transformed water into wine at the wedding in Cana, God transforms our hearts and our lives. My faith goal is: "Mess with the mind in order to organize the heart" (*Easum and Bandy*).

Wright

At what point did you accept God's call and how did you feel?

Carter

I'll be honest—I've been running away from God for about twenty years and before I accepted the call I never intended to ever be in a church—ever in my life. I went to church as a kid, off and on. I attended a church school, but I had this idea that at some point church folks were real hypocrites. They said one thing and did something else, which made me believe somehow that their God was not that powerful. So, when I accepted the call in 1991, I'll be honest, it scared me to death. I was working in a prison as a warden's assistant when the call came and I really tried to run.

Wright

So God wanted you to be in the ministry and you didn't and you thought He had no sense of humor.

Carter

When God called me, I could not believe it. It was weird. My husband and I were riding down the street and he said, "What are you going to do with the next five years of your life?" I said, "Be a minister." As soon as I said that, I looked at him and he looked at me and we both shut up. (Neither one of us were church goers at the time.)

Those of us who are Christians know God has a great sense of humor. God calls those who are the least likely candidates to ministry. God spends time pruning us and equipping us with life's experiences from the day we are born. Does God have a sense of humor? Sure God does—He called *me!*

Wright

So was there any specific event in your life that led you into the ministry?

Carter

I think every event in my life has led me to ministry. As I look back into the annals of my mind, I don't know if it was the physical abuse I suffered under the hands of my mother or the sexual abuse experienced at the hands of a friend of the family. Whether it was being a pregnant teen at the age of fourteen (in a time when it was unacceptable) or whether it was the loneliness and loss I felt at my father's disappearance from the family. If I tried to separate these events, it would not be possible. I believe I was called to these events.

These events provided an opportunity for me to become a counselor, member of the clergy, and Christian.

My call was and still is to help others get from under the same devastation I had already suffered. Now, do not get me wrong—I am not one of those persons who believe one must be a drug addict in order to help someone who is, but you sure have to know something about pain. Pain led me to ministry. As a Christian, I am called to assist God in alleviating people's pain. How do I assist? Simple—I tell others about God and I live a life with intimate expectation and with faith.

I think every event in my life has led me to ministry.

Wright

You know, it's interesting to note (at least as I read it) that Jesus must have been really charismatic. To draw 15,000 people or even 5,000 people to a service on a hillside—people following Him all over the place—He must have had some great attributes. The only question I can remember the disciples ever asking Him was to teach them to pray. They must have thought that was very powerful. How important is prayer when it comes to faith, in your opinion?

Carter

Prayer is the quintessential element of intimacy with God. When Jesus was in the Garden of Gethsemane approaching His final hour He was found praying. When He was on the cross, He was in conversation with God. Prayer is everything. Communicating with God and having God communicate back is what life is all about.

Prayer is one of our calls to worship. Prayer helps us reach the unreachable and touch people who are considered untouchable. It is through prayer that people are healed, that lives are transformed, and our faith is renewed.

Wright

Has there ever been a point in your life when you felt that God was not listening?

Carter

All through my childhood, and during some of my adulthood, I felt stuck in a vacuum without any assistance. It seemed that God had left me by myself to figure out life. I thought that when I needed God, He was busy with someone else.

One of my favorite stories by Bruce Wilkinson is *The Prayer of Jabez*. Jabez (in Hebrew *Ya'vetz* or *Ya'betz*) means "sorrow," deriving from a root word meaning "to grieve." The word *ya'betz* and the term for pain (*ozeb*) sound alike, though the letters in *ozeb* are in reverse order. This Hebrew pun on the word "pain" is used as a tool to explain the circumstances of the child's birth. Pain had always been my first, middle, and last name. I didn't know anything different existed.

It is interesting that the more often pain knocked on my door and made an entrance, the more God called my name. I wanted to know this God. Even if He was going to ignore me, I still screamed and searched for this illusive God. I still called on God's name.

I also learned about pain from another biblical character named Job. Because of my experiences with some of life's suffering, I have always identified with Job. Job lost his children, his livelihood, his friends, and even his health. Job is as man after my own heart. No matter what he experienced in life, he did not lose his faith in God.

Wright

Obviously you've experienced quite a bit of suffering in your life. How do you reconcile the pain you have felt with issues of hope, love, and faith?

Carter

I think love is everything—I think love for the Creator, love for one another—we are a connected responsibility. I think we have a responsibility to one another to care for one another, to love one another, and to help one another move to the next phase of life.

I think that pain does not necessarily have to last for the rest of your days. I am a firm believer in not allowing other people to define who you are based upon the circumstances of your life. Whether rich, poor, black, white, pink, or green, it doesn't matter. God is a God of love and if we allow ourselves to step out on this word—if we allow ourselves to believe in a Power that says, "Listen, you know what? You can talk to a mountain and it will move, just trust me, have some faith in me," we can then experience that hope.

I have hope every day when I wake up and I work with people in all walks of life, from working with children in juvenile detention centers to working with inmates in prisons to working in the area of mental health, or children's services. People are always looking for that sense of hope; they need to know people love them. They also need to know that God loves them as well. I look at pain and I say,

"Okay, you can get over this—you can get past this—you cannot allow it to define who you are."

Wright

If you could wave a magic wand, would you change any of the events in your life that led you to this point?

Carter

No. And that may be an unusual answer. The events of my past and present have made me who I am. The choices made in wisdom or without have caused me to seek a God, who, like an erupting volcano or a gentle breeze, causes my life to shift, to change direction for good.

God has been able to use everything that I have ever gone through to help someone else. For example, I lived in a shelter for the homeless for about a month. I was working with the developmentally disabled as a group home administrator, living in one city and working in another. Previously someone offered me a house in Columbus, Ohio, to live in. So, I closed out my apartment, packed up my three children and headed for Columbus from Dayton (about three hours away). As Satan would have it, before I arrived at the house, it caught on fire and burned to the ground. Being unfamiliar with the area, I was at a loss as to where to go. My children and I spent a couple of nights in a rest area, a couple of nights at someone's house, and for two weeks, we slept in my car. Okay. That sounds like a miserable story, right? Not so. God did an interesting thing. He encouraged me to hire some of the women who were living in that shelter—women who had not had jobs in years and years. They needed a boost. They needed to know that they were lovable and loved and that they were worthy of being alive.

I do not want anyone to get the impression that I was happy being at that shelter—not at all—in fact, I was miserable. However, God knew what everyone needed. The women needed to feel like human beings again. God had the key; He provided me with the door. These events taught me the following:

- The importance of faith and what it means to be completely dependent upon God.
- We all have a purpose in life; it is important to ask God what it is.
- People are hurting everywhere; God has given us His grace to help them.

- Without forgiveness we torture ourselves, cause others and ourselves pain. Without forgiveness we lose, continuing to give others power over us.
- Hope, love, and faith function as stress relievers offering us life free from fear.

Wright

So what do you say to people who seem to have lost all hope in their own lives?

Carter

I challenge them to choose to win and not to lose. Trusting in God helps us destroy old tapes about being unworthy. Parents, friends, and all the people we meet have an opinion about who we are and who we are not. Some of us are so wounded that at the age of forty we are still suffering from the hurtful words spoken to us when we were five. Without hope, we keep reliving the pain. Pain has a way of keeping us focused on the negative. For example: Some of us could be given thunderous applause at an event and then we would focus on the one person who did not clap. God made us to be winners—more than conquerors. We are made in God's image, meaning we are strong and courageous—we are beautiful.

If we choose to win then we will take time to learn from our experiences. We will take time to grow from our past instead of having events keep us frozen in fear.

We are supposed to be a connected people. It is our responsibility to help people choose life over death. We can get over anything with God's help—we just have to believe in God strong enough. Our mission is to love God and know that we are God's children. We are to also love one another. Hope, love, and faith are the main ingredients to a life worth living.

Wright

So I understand you have a nickname, how did you get it?

Carter

My nickname is "Pure Love." I am amazed people actually call me that. Years ago, one of my friends was trying to describe me to someone. He was talking about my love for humanity, for God, and for the work I do in the community. They were asking him how someone who had experienced so much pain in her life could be as pleasant as I was. They wanted to know how I maintained my attitude of love and respect for others. He said, "She is pure love. She believes in the love of humanity and love for humanity. Her faith keeps her strong. She's just pure love!" It stuck and so people call me that.

Wright

So what does that nickname have to do with your ministry today?

Carter

Jesus Christ is pure love. I try to live my life in a way that would be pleasing to Him—loving other people unconditionally, even if I don't understand them, even in spite of myself. Sometimes I think people are worth loving and I think people need to know they are truly loved by somebody. I don't think that as a human being I have a right to judge who to love and who not to. We all need love and we need it unconditionally.

Wright

As you look back on your life—the good and the bad—what do you think your biggest accomplishments have been?

Carter

My biggest accomplishment has been being able to understand myself as God has created me—being able to throw out old tapes, think positively about life, and be able to identify who I am in Christ. I guess initially, when others think about accomplishments, they think about academic degrees, although important, they are not everything. My biggest accomplishments have been helping people love themselves while helping them understand that love does not have to hurt.

Wright

Well, can I ask you one final question? When I was reading your introduction, it said that you challenge your audiences not to be defined by circumstances or by the choices they make. I can understand your advice to not be defined by our circumstances, but I've always been taught that we are a combination of the choices we make. You say we are not defined by our choices. What do you mean by that?

Carter

I don't think we are defined by our choices. I think our choices are important and certainly they can tend to define what we do. For example, I guess the biggest example for me is that I have diabetes. I always hate saying that I'm a diabetic because I'm not that. I'm me, with a disease—with diabetes. People who drink too much, for example, are called alcoholics but that's not how God defines them—they're a person who has made the choice to drink, for whatever reason, but they're not that choice. I agree we are the sum of our experiences and that includes some of the choices we make, but God says we are made in His image—in the image of love and trust and forgiveness and compassion. So I don't see us being our choice. We can *make* a choice, but it doesn't define who we are, it just means we've made that choice.

Wright

Very interesting. Well, what a great conversation, I've learned a lot here today and I really do appreciate your taking all this time with me.

Today we have been talking with the Reverend Desiree Carter who is a pastor. Her life's journeys and experiences have called her to provide self-esteem, life skills, stress relief training, team building, and how to manage conflict to both individuals and corporations. As a motivational speaker, Desiree educates, inspires, and empowers her audiences to take risks choosing growth over fear. I think we've found out here that she really knows what she's talking about, at least *I* think she does.

Desiree, thank you so much for being with us today on *Speaking of Faith!*

Carter

David, thank you very much for inviting me to be a part of this project.

About The Author

DESIREE CARTER is an ordained minister and speaker who uses her skills, education, and life's experiences to educate and empower others to succeed in business and life. Known as "the Life Force Mechanic," she has over twenty years experience challenging her audiences to look in the mirror and see the stranger within. During her seminars and workshops Desiree helps her audiences decode their experiences of the past in order to repair the problems of present, creating avenues of growth and success in both business and significant relationships of the future.

Desiree's motto: Empowerment in life begins with your choices in life. Her message: In order to succeed at anything we must first know who we are. The next time you go by a mirror, stop, look in it and ask yourself this question: "Who Am I?"

Desiree is a member of the National Speakers Association. She graduated from The Methodist Theological School of Ohio with a Master's degree in Divinity and a Master's degree in Alcohol and Substance Abuse ministry. She holds a Bachelor of Arts degree in Vocational Rehabilitation, and a Bachelor of Arts in Sociology from Wilberforce University, in Wilberforce, Ohio.

Desiree is an Elder serving the West Ohio Conference of the United Methodist church. She also serves as pastor of St. Paul's United Methodist Church in Toledo, Ohio.

Desiree Carter

Mirror Image Consulting

2227 Densmore Drive

Toledo, Ohio 43606

Phone: 419.536.3456

Chapter 11

Victoria McArthur

THE INTERVIEW

David Wright (Wright)

Today we're talking with Victoria McArthur. She is a mother, business owner, consultant, interior decorator, designer, realtor, and writer who tries to seek ways to assist others, not just in food and clothing, but in ways that help make others feel good about themselves and to help them share God's blessings with others. "We are here on earth to be God's eyes, ears, mouth, hands, and feet," says Victoria. "We are here in the flesh and He is here in the Spirit to guide us."

Victoria McArthur, welcome to *Speaking of Faith*.

Victoria McArthur (McArthur)

Thank you so much. This is such a blessing to me.

Wright

Let me ask you right up front: what kind of childhood do you think your mother had and why do you think your mother joined the Navy as a young wife? How did she react to that?

McArthur

My mother had a very hard childhood. Her parents separated and the two sisters were separated. Mother went to live with my grandmother. My Aunt went to live with my grandfather. That was during the Depression so they had hand-me-down clothes. My Mother was especially upset over the other children laughing at her clothing—she never forgot. They were told they were lucky they even had shoes. They had very little food but they survived. Grandmother tried to work and do the best she could. Eventually, after five years, she and my grandfather decided to live together because of the girls who were going astray. They started focusing on their children rather than their own likes or dislikes.

As a young woman, Mother married my father who was going off to World War II. Mother wanted to do something for her country but had never been away from home. She decided to join the Navy and loved it. She made many friends and she thought my dad would be so proud of her. Unfortunately, she did this without my dad knowing it. My dad was the type of person who wanted total control, so he was not happy. Through the course of letters and phone calls, he upset my mother to the point where she had a nervous breakdown. She was able to obtain an honorable discharge and was released from the hospital to come home. Up until then she loved the Navy.

I will say this: the Veterans Hospital in Gainesville was wonderful to us during her life and until the end. I owe them a lot of thanks.

Wright

So were you born when she went into the Navy or was that before you were born?

McArthur

No, I was not born until after the War was over—I was one of the "war babies." My parents were married about five years before I came along.

Wright

Why do you think your mother had trouble understanding the Bible and misinterpreted the Word?

McArthur

I think Mother went the way of the world to a point because of her parents being separated. I think she was always searching. I think that when she started reading the Bible she found out she had done things that were wrong and she wanted to be forgiven. However. I don't think she applied the part of the Bible that said God would forgive her if she would go to Him and talk to Him about her sins and the things she had done in her life. She could never let go of the guilt—she kept it with her almost up until the day she died. It was a discussion she and I would have and I told her to let it go, "The Lord has forgiven you."

When studying the Bible she got very engrossed in it. Her way of giving to the Lord was that Mother and I would sometimes walk to church—we would "suffer" walking to church—and as far as she was concerned, that was our way of showing the Lord we loved Him.

She would go overboard. When I would come to her and say something to her such as, "Do you care if I go down to a friend's house?" Mother would turn to me and she would say, "The Lord will protect you; you go on." As a child growing up, I didn't want to hear that. I wanted to hear my mother say, "Yes, go ahead. Be back in an hour." Mother just took her religion to heart. When speakers would come to the church, she would have them stay at the house. She was always trying to do everything perfectly because that was her way of being Christian.

Mother had a very gentle spirit when she was younger. She really just tried very hard to live the right way; but I don't believe she could ever forgive herself for her sins.

Wright

So why did your mother struggle most of her life? Was it due to all her illnesses?

McArthur

I believe it was. Her past bothered her—she was always afraid that people who knew her past might say something to my dad that would upset him. She could never let go of it and I think her breakdown when she was in the service followed her a lot.

My dad was a very, very strong man. He was a very controlling person. He kept her under his thumb—that was his way of control. If Mother wanted to take a college course or something, he wouldn't allow it. We did not know at the time what her problem was but it was steadily taking control.

Mother had another breakdown when I was about ten years old and I still remember going to the psychiatric ward in the Methodist

Hospital in Indianapolis to visit her. They did those terrible shock treatments back then on her. As a young child, I remember walking into the hospital room and seeing my mother held down by two male nurses and a lady nurse. Mother had tried to get to the window to jump out and commit suicide because of the treatments. That was a very hard thing for me as a child to experience—to see my Mother asking to die—no one had ever told me she was schizophrenic. About ten years later Mother went to the Marion Indiana Hospital. For a short time they called her condition a "chemical imbalance" (this is what my dad called it).

Wright
Is that your first memory of her illness?

McArthur
Yes.

Wright
What affect did it have on you?

McArthur
One time I was at my grandmother's house and I remember watching my mother try to walk across the room. She shook so violently she couldn't even make it across the room. I remember asking my grandmother, "What's going on?" A young child doesn't understand this.

My grandmother said, "Well, your mother has read the Bible and she has misinterpreted it and it just got her all upset and she's had a breakdown over it." What that did to me was to turn me against God and the Bible because I didn't want to be like my mother. I did not want to study something that was going to put me in a situation where I was as ill as my mother was.

Because of her illness she was just not there as a mother. I was raised 80 percent of the time by my grandmother who was a very loving, outreaching woman. She thought of me as her daughter. If something nice can be found in all this, it was that when Mother was in the mental institution in Indianapolis I became closer to my grandmother. I made the adjustment of living with her; it wasn't a hard adjustment to be with my grandmother. I was not tossed from being at home and then somewhere else. It was an easier way for me. Mother knew I was being taken care of. I adored my grandmother and Mother knew her mother would be good to me. My mother cared, she just didn't know how to show her love.

I will say this about my dad: he stood by my mother throughout her illness. He never wavered. My father also had a hard life growing up and my mother was too sick to stand up to him. He allowed me to live with my grandmother because he was a fireman and on the job twenty-four hours and off twenty-four hours. That was not a good schedule for a little girl.

Wright

So, why do you think you went the way of the world instead of the way of the Lord?

McArthur

I think it was because of watching my mother. We were brought up in church. We went to a very strict Baptist church where you would go in and barely speak to anybody and Lord have mercy if anyone said, "Amen," during the service!

As a child I was never allowed to show emotions in front of my parents. If I started to cry they would say, "That's enough of that," and I would stop. I was never kissed goodnight and tucked into bed when I was little. It was very lonely never being able to express my feelings. I have been accused of being cold. A few years before her death my mother said they had brought me up in a cold environment. My grandmother was the only person who showed me loving warmth.

My mother sort of pushed me into getting married when I was seventeen years old. I was not near old enough for that kind of major life change. I could never understand why she wanted to do this. But my husband was from a good family and Mother wanted me to be around good people and in a good family. I never knew that this was a part of her illness because I was raised in it. I didn't know what was normal and what wasn't.

That marriage didn't last because I was just too young and so was the father of my children. We just went our own way. So I ran from Christianity and I lived the song, "Looking for Love in all the Wrong Places." It took me a lot of hardship before I stopped. I had to grow up.

But I will tell you this: through all my trials and tribulations Mother and Dad were always there for me. They might not have liked my divorce but they were there to help with the children. I wanted to start a business. I knew I could succeed but I did not have the money.

They lent me the money to start my business and I was able to pay them back in three months.

They were good in many ways, but what I really needed was warmth. They weren't able to give that to me, yet they were able to do it for my children and for that I am very thankful. My children love and respected my parents and spent an enormous amount of time with them. My children will tell you that they had the best grandparents in the world; there were none any better than theirs.

During all this, Mother had had several breakdowns. One time we had a doctor tell my dad he needed to divorce my mother because the doctor didn't believe he could get my mother out of the state of mind she was in. He said that if she did recover and had another breakdown, she would never come out of an institution. My dad and I sat down and talked about it for a long time. He did not divorce my mother, he stayed with her, which was a blessing; but he always held this over her and told her if she crossed him he would leave.

I told her that I would take care of her and she should let him go (knowing that he would not go too far).

One time, after a problem with my father my mother said she got a gun, put it to her head but did not know how to take off the manual safety device. I got so upset with her I said, "What do you think that would do to me to find you like that?" Mother then told me she could not do it because she wanted to go to heaven and she knew that God would not approve, so she could not do it.

(At the time of my mother's funeral my father was beginning to show symptoms of Alzheimer's disease.) On the way to Mother's funeral, as I was driving the car, my father told me that he and Mom had never had an argument. I almost wrecked the car in shock!

One day, about a year before Mother died, she was having a terrible reaction. We were trying to get her off some medicine that doctors had prescribed many years prior. We were at the hospital and she came in shaking terribly. It was horrible to see her like that.

Through that whole experience, the Lord had put many angels in my way. I didn't know they were angels until I could later on look back and realize they had been with me. God always had His hand on me but I was going to do it my way. I had to learn the hard way. For me that was really a blessing because since I learned the hard way, perhaps I can help someone else not go that way. I've already "been there done that" and I would never want to go back. That way is dark—not thinking of others and always picking the wrong people to be with. The devil can get a hold on you and make all things look great, whether they're good for you or not. Finally I talked to a Christian doctor who helped me see differently.

Wright

So you really do feel that there are angels here on the earth?

McArthur

Oh, most definitely. When I was at the hospital waiting room there was a gentleman sitting nearby who was looking at me. He could tell I was very distraught because I had been going through a difficult time with my mother for months. Being the only child, I was the one they called every time something went wrong. I was sitting there almost in tears—it was just overwhelming. This gentleman, whose name was Ray Ragsdale, looked at me and said, "Are you having a bad day today?"

I said, "Yes. It's very hard—I don't know what's wrong with my mother and I'm just so distraught." I was almost in tears; my face must have had fear written on it.

"I write poems," Ray said. "Some of them have been published."

"Oh, really?" I said. To be honest, I wasn't in the mood to hear this; but he was really a very nice gentleman.

"I have a poem for you and I want to give it to you," he said.

Just what I wanted. I couldn't see. I felt terrible. I could hardly read it.

The poem was about angels and went:

God has angels here on earth to help us along the way.
With loving smiles and tender words, they brighten up our day.
They always think of others and help us through many things.
We just don't know who they are because we can't see their wings.

He was there that day to help me. I know that now.

This struck me so hard that I looked at him and realized I really needed that—at that particular moment I needed an angel. This is the poem I had someone read at my mother's funeral because it meant so much to me—that someone cared. So, yes, I believe there are angels on earth. We just have to be in tuned to them.

We were studying in our Bible group about giving to the less fortunate. We decided that we should give food not money when we helped. God said, "If they were hungry we should feed them." We did not want to help them with money because some would use the money to purchase alcohol or cigarettes.

One day I was going to have my nails done. I like to get a Coke prior to that. I noticed a poorly dressed man who was sitting alone. I prayed silently, "Dear Lord, why do you always put them in my path? I get upset and I'm not sure what to do." I went to the counter and bought a Coke and on the way out I stopped and asked the gentlemen if he had eaten.

He looked up at me and smiled with the most gorgeous set of teeth that were as white as snow. "Yes, I have. I had a hamburger and Coke," he said.

I then asked if he was all right and he said he was.

The next week at Bible study I was sharing the incident with the Bible study Group and they started to laugh. They said he was probably someone who had lots of money and I had asked him if he was hungry. He had probably had a big laugh. I did it with the right intention. Who was right?

One of my angels is Joni Tabor who I know you have interviewed. The reason I say she is one of my angels is because Joni and I are very close. We are "sisters." Finally, after fifty-nine years I have a sister in my life. She travels to give testimony to God's glory by performing singing concerts and giving inspirational talks. She always stays with us when she visits my church. After Mother's death I was talking with Joni. I told her that one night the Lord woke me up and said He would like for me to write a book about my mother. My reaction was, "Yeah, right—I don't know anything about doing that. If you want me to Lord, you have to do it."

Joni said, "Well, you just never know."

"If it's the Lord's will," I said, "it will happen. I don't know how to get started but if I can help any one person with what I went through because of my mother, that's what I would like to do." And here I am now talking with you today. I will tell you, this is the Lord's will in my life—to tell my story about the way I was going, what happened during my mother's illness and her last year, and now with Dad and his Alzheimer's disease.

Mother was five feet, four inches and weighed two hundred pounds. On one trip to the hospital the doctor said they wanted to put her in nursing home rehabilitation for a month, so mother agreed.

After she went into the nursing home I started seeing things going wrong. She heard people talking about her, and started seeing things; it was terrible. Then one day I got a call from the nursing home to come and get Mother—she had locked herself in the bathroom, trashed a bed, and pulled a light off the wall. I had no choice. I had to take Mother to the hospital to find out what caused this behavior.

During my mother's last year she was "BakerActed." To be Baker-Acted is to be committed into a mental hospital involuntarily—you have no control at all. BakerActed patients can be sent wherever the State wants to send them, they can do what they want and the family has no control.

When Mother was BakerActed I thought I was going to lose *my* mind! I was just appalled. I got into a big argument with the doctor. He was right though—Mother didn't know what was going on; she was very ill. When they put her in the hospital she was sent to the VA hospital in Gainesville. They were very, very good to her.

What she went through and what I went through watching her was very difficult at the time but is now a blessing because the Lord showed me her illness and what it really was. As a child I didn't understand or accept it. As an adult I had to live with it with her. It was horrifying when the doctor came out and told me that my mother was bipolar and schizophrenic. The look on my face was one of such distress. I had never heard that said about my mother.

For three days Mother was in the mental health ward of the VA hospital. We could not go to see her. She tried to escape and fell. I would call and I would hear her screaming. It makes me sick even to write this. Finally they let Dad and me go in and Mother was running her hands through her food saying that they were trying to kill her. Dad and I went there every day. My daughter Melissa flew down from Indiana to see her. I tried to tell her how hard it was to see Mother like this. When Melissa went in to see her grandmother she stayed only about fifteen minutes. She then came out and told me she needed to go out for a minute. Melissa had such a hard time and was so upset that the nurse had to talk to her and help her. She saw for the first time what Dad and I were going through.

Melissa called her brother, Lance, to tell him about her experience with their grandmother. She kept saying, "You don't know how bad it is to see our grandmother like this. It is just awful." Lance kept telling her he knew and she kept saying, "You don't know, you have to be here."

Mother would lie in bed 90 percent of the time and maybe one day a month she would have a good day. Her ear hurt, her foot hurt—there was always something with Mother. I got tired of hearing it. In fact, unfortunately, they "cry wolf" so much, that when the "wolf" is actually at the door you don't pay any attention.

When they told me Mother was schizophrenic and bipolar I couldn't believe it. I had taken my mother to my family physician who is a very good internist. He asked me if she was schizophrenic when he saw one of the medicines she was taking. I told him, "Heavens no! She's not schizophrenic." I turned and said "Mother, are you schizophrenic?" She hadn't heard that term and wondered why they had her on medicine that was for the treatment of schizophrenics. It was a very terrible medicine—in fact, they don't even prescribe it anymore.

Wright

Do you believe that someone with a mental health problem can still have faith?

McArthur

Oh, most definitely. I believe that if someone will take time just to talk with a person with mental problems, they can have faith. When my mother was BakerActed, she was in the emergency room. They finally allowed me to go in to see her. She was sitting up on the bed with her feet on the edge of the bed swinging them back and forth.

"Mother, what's going on?" I asked

"Well," she said, in a very upbeat voice, "I have decided something. I have decided that the Lord has allowed me to suffer all these years so I can be a testimony to Him."

There she was, seventy-nine years old, swinging her feet like a five-year-old child. I said, "Do you really think so, Mother?"

"Oh, yes. I most definitely do."

A nurse came around to check on Mother and Mother said to her, "Do you believe? Are you a Christian?"

The nurse replied, "Yes, I am."

Mother said, "If you're a Christian I'll allow you to help me. If you're not, I don't want you to."

My husband has said, "Oh, now, she wasn't in her right mind." I say you can put it any way you want to but, until the day she died, she would call me and ask me, "Would you pray that I will die? I want to go home and be with the Lord and I want to be with my mother."

I would ask her, "Are you praying out loud to the Lord? Don't pray inside—pray out loud and tell Him you want to go home." She told me she was and I told her, "Then He'll take you home but it has to be in His time." I agreed to pray for her to go home.

Because of Mother being BakerActed, no one would take her. The nursing homes would read her file and see that she was schizophrenic and even though she was on medication, no one would take her. I tried to check this out myself. I called and I visited nursing homes. I checked them out and did everything I could. The VA hospital was pressuring me to get her out of there. I was trying and trying and finally one day I yelled to the Lord, "Lord, I've done everything I can do—I need Your help! I need You to find a place for my mother. I can not do it alone!" The next day I received a phone call and was able to place Mother—not where I wanted to place her but a nursing home was willing to take her.

The night before she passed away the Lord woke me up and I wondered if I should drive over to see her. It was about a twenty-minute drive and it was four in the morning. I really didn't want to drive that lonely road by myself. I prayed saying, "Lord, I'm really asking You to take her home. It says in Your Word if I come to You and ask You, You will honor that. You know she wants to come home. You know she doesn't want to be there and that she has a terrible life. I love her enough to let her go. Please take her home to be with You." I did not make the drive; I called and they said Mother was sleeping. I did not need to come over.

The next day I went shopping with my girlfriend. It was the day after Thanksgiving; we always go shopping on that. I received a phone call telling me I should go to the nursing home. I went immediately and called my husband. I asked him to pick up my dad and bring him to the nursing home. We were there for several hours not knowing. I sat with her and held her hand and started to cry and I remember saying, "I'm sorry Mother. I know you don't like me to cry," and a tear rolled down her face. She passed away while I was holding her hand. She looked so peaceful.

I know the Lord had His hand in all this. He had to wake me up to her illness. He had to show me the whole way because I was going to do it on my terms; but He brought me to my knees.

Wright

So, why are you telling about her faith in God?

McArthur

Because I think there are many people out there who are mentally challenged. I think Christians don't realize they need to talk with these people about Christ—they don't think mentally challenged people will understand. I believe that if at any time in their life they had faith, I think it's still there. I think the Lord always has His hand on them; but He also has His hand on others to go talk with them. You can't carry on a conversation with them as you would with what we would call "normal" people but you can reach them.

My father has Alzheimer's disease. He and I talk about the Lord and sometimes I take him to church. He also attends church services where he lives. His body is there but his mind is not there. When I take him to our church service he doesn't always comprehend but I will ask him, "Dad, do you still believe in Jesus Christ?" and he will answer, "Yes."

He and I were baptized together. I was baptized when I was a young child—my mother pushed me into it. I did not realize the full meaning of being baptized. I was baptized again when I was an adult.

My dad didn't attend church regularly. Mother and Dad were brought up to believe that if you do good and live a good life then you automatically go to heaven.

I believe that there are a lot of people out there who have mental problems and Christians don't take the time to talk with them about faith. If my mother's story would help just one person then the life she lived would be so rich. I would like to tell her story.

Wright

So why do you think God would choose to take this time so late in your life to help you understand and forgive her?

McArthur

I think that I held it against her because she was not a mother I could go to. I think I resented that Mother never knew me. When she was in the hospital, she would say to me, "If anything happens to me, I want you to take care of your father." That always bothered me because what kind of a Christian wouldn't take care of their father? I would take care of Mother because that was the right thing to do— biblically I had to do what was right. I was closer to my grandmother and loved my grandmother. Mother was not a mother image to me. Mother didn't teach me the things a mother teaches her little girl. She would be harsh—Mother could be mean. I never understood that it was a result of her illness. The Lord gave me a blessing by letting me see how she did suffer. She suffered and I suffered. My friends could see me suffering. What it did was make me turn to the Lord. He would let me know He was with me the whole time but I couldn't see it at the time.

Wright

What an interesting conversation and an enlightening one as well. I guess all of us have these kinds of situations in our past. Stories like yours remind us of things that have happened and give us the courage to look at them as they are, learn from them, and be better people.

I really appreciate the time you've taken to answer these personal questions.

McArthur

I'm so honored that this has happened. I praise God that He has given me this opportunity. It's through Him that this has all taken place. The wonder is that He has opened my eyes and has let me see things.

I would like to say something else in closing. Paul wrote in his second letter to Timothy, "I have fought a good fight, I have finished my course, I have kept the faith . . . " (2 Timothy 4:7). Mother had finished the race and she kept the faith. I think God granted me the realization of how much I really, truly loved my mother, and I didn't know I did.

Wright

She will be glad to know that her children are rising up and thanking God for her presence.

Today we've been talking with Victoria McArthur about the life and the trials and tribulations of her mother and in some ways her entire family. I think by listening and by reading this book, you, the reader, have been able to gain a lot of insight into how God works in the lives of all of us.

Thank you, Victoria, for being with us on *Speaking of Faith*.

The Books

From the time we are born, our life becomes a book.
With all events recorded there, from the first breath we took.
Listing each and every work, from the time we first talked.
Showing every step we took, and down which path we walked.
The pages there give account, of all the things we know;
Everything good and bad, and if we were being true.
As we grow the pages show, everything we do each day,
The happiness and anger, in the things we do and say.
Written on these pages, is our life from the start,
Not only what we do and say, but what is in our heart.
There is another, greater Book, where our names may be written.
It doesn't list the good or bad, it's a list of those forgiven.
By Ray C. Ragsdale

This man was an angel in my life in my day of need.

A Daughter's Remembrance of Her Mother

My mother's struggle to live a normal life became harder for her as she was misdiagnosed by her family.

As a daughter, no one shared her condition with me and if my father knew, he did not tell me (I really do not think he knew). The only person who hinted at it was my grandmother who said that Mother was very sick.

My mother never gave up her faith and believed, even during the bad times, which were many. She was a quiet person, meek and mild most of her life. She was very submissive until near the end when she became violent and hateful at times, then retreated back to being meek and quiet.

All of our lives were very stressful, especially not knowing her correct diagnosis. By the time we were told she was bipolar and had schizophrenia, and tried to understand all of the previous concerns, she was extremely ill.

One very stressful day, when the doctor had BakerActed Mother, she was sitting on the side of the bed, swinging her legs and proclaiming Jesus Christ to everyone.

This was the day I learned to put everything in God's hands. Due to the Baker Act and all of Mother's illnesses, none of the patient care facilities would take her. I begged and pleaded but to no avail. I prayed to God and asked for His help. He led me to Williston where they took her in.

She asked me to pray that God would take her home to be with Him and to see her mother. I went on my knees and prayed that He would relieve her pain and suffering. God answered my prayers. I thank God daily for His help and understanding.

My final evaluation was from God to understand that how Mother struggled all her life with her illness was through prayer.

Victoria McArthur
August 24, 2005

Acknowledgements:

I want to thank God for His unconditional love.

I want to thank God for my parents and for showing me that He is always with us.

I want to thank my children for the love they have always shown their grandparents and the time they spent together.

I want to thank my husband for loving me unconditionally— without God in our lives we would never have met.

I want to thank my secretary for her time and devotion to our family. She has always been there for me.

I want to thank my husband's children who are very special to me for accepting me into their lives.

To God be the glory.

About The Author

Victoria McArthur is a mother, business owner, consultant, interior decorator, designer, realtor, and writer who tries to seek ways to assist others in different ways—not just in food and clothing, but in ways that help make others feel good about themselves and to help them share God's blessings with others. "We are here on earth to be God's eyes, ears, mouth, hands, and feet," says Victoria. "We are here in the flesh and He is here in the Spirit to guide us."

Victoria McArthur
3501 W. University Avenue, Suite D-1
Gainesville, FL 32607
352-378-7041

Chapter 12

REV. DR. CHARLOTTE B. PETTY

David Wright (Wright)

Today we're talking with the Reverend Dr. Charlotte B. Petty. Dr. Petty considers it important to know what she believes and why. Her life is dedicated to impart divine truths into the life of others. She challenges traditional thinking, encouraging others to expand their views.

It has been said, "We only believe that which we do." Dr. Petty is a prominent Christian leader. She truly lives what she talks about. She is the pastor of a growing congregation and serves as District Elder and Lay Director of the Western Region of the Pentecostal Assemblies of the World, Inc.

Dr. Petty, welcome to our program, *Speaking of Faith.*

Rev. Dr. Charlotte B. Petty (Petty)

Thank you.

Wright

Speaking of faith, how do you define faith?

Petty

As a born again Christian my definition of faith has to come from God's point of view. I embrace *The Message* version of Hebrews 11:1, "The fundamental fact of existence is that this trust in God, this faith, is the firm foundation under everything that makes life worth living. It's our handle on what we can't see." So to me the application of faith is having an attitude that my whole life is entrusted in Christ—every phase of it.

As a believer, my purpose in life is to please God. In Hebrews 11:6 it states, "It's impossible to please God apart from faith. And why? Because anyone who wants to approach God must believe both that he exists and that he cares enough to respond to those who seek Him."

An important point about faith is that it is only as good as the object in which it is placed. I am one among many who reads the Bible but I need to apply it to myself. In Romans 10:17 I read, "So then faith cometh by hearing, and hearing by the word of God" (KJV).

One of the examples that helped me a lot was the story of Abraham and Isaac. I was so intrigued because God told Abraham to sacrifice Isaac. Abraham took Isaac and left his other people behind. Isaac even asked him, "Dad, where is the sacrifice?"

Abraham responded, "God will provide."

But Abraham continued to do as God had requested. As he laid Isaac on the altar and raised the knife in his hand, God said, "Hold it." As the story goes, there was a ram caught in the bush nearby. The part I'm excited about is this: "Faith cometh by hearing," and it doesn't say it comes by what you heard. This means that I have to keep an open ear; for example, the direction of God may be, "Charlotte, move north." But while I'm moving north, I've got to be listening because He may tell me to go northeast or northwest instead of straight north. This has been a source in my life—to rely on a *daily* walk with God. It has caused me to have a *lifestyle* of faith, not just something that happens today and that's it. I live and breathe a faith walk.

Wright

Is having faith enough? Where does taking personal responsibility or making a contribution to society fit in?

Petty

No, I don't believe faith is enough. I have a Bible basis for that because it says in James 2:20 and James 2:26 that, "Faith without works is dead." The one thing I strongly believe is that if I have faith I have to act on it. Faith means acting as if it's already done. What happens is this: You can say, "I believe my car will take me to Tacoma." And I can say, "I believe my car will take me to Tacoma," all I want to, but I will never move from the spot I am in unless I put the key in the ignition, turn it on, and move the car—press on the accelerator. So I realize I have to believe in a God who can do anything, but I must listen and move in the direction I need to move in.

In the society I live in I have a responsibility to make it a better place. We talk about separation of church and state but I believe that the church is not a building, the church is a body—I am the church. I'm in the world and because I'm here I must make a positive contribution to my community, I must get involved. People must be able to see Jesus through me or any child of God, so I must be that example and the person who makes a contribution.

Last week I had the opportunity of joining in with Washington State law enforcement officers in a conference. The purpose of the conference was to show that faith organizations and our law enforcement both need to partner in order to help our community be a better place to live. So I honestly believe, as a child of God and having faith and trust in Him, that I also need to exhibit this in my society.

Wright

How did your parents impact your faith as a lifestyle?

Petty

My parents are Christians but I often tell people that my parents created within me an appetite for living the way I live. My mother had twelve children and she was a stay-at-home mom. I'm child number two and I did not have the responsibility of taking care of my brothers and sisters because Mom would not let us touch our siblings as infants until they were walking.

My mother was a praying woman. I didn't even know that there was a doctor until I was eighteen years old because when anything happened to me—if I would get sick—my mother would pray for me. And do you know what? I got well. So I believe I have faith in God as a healer.

We didn't have all the conveniences other children had. I didn't have an allowance. I belonged to a large church and we would have youth meetings outside of Detroit and I would want to go. My parents didn't have the money to give to me. My mother would tell me, "Why don't you ask the Lord?" I would get on my knees and pray and it would come to me to share that need with someone. I would go to my uncle (or whomever I was impressed to go to) and I would say something like, "Uncle Wilson, the youth are going such-and-such a place and I really would like to go," and he would give me the money to go. I would go on a three-day trip in those days with fifty cents in my pocket and would come back home with my fifty cents. I ate three meals and slept in a warm bed at night. In those days you didn't go to hotels, you went to people's homes when you traveled. My mother and father were examples to me of faith and they made God real to me. I experienced Him for myself.

As a youngster I would go to my mom and say, "Mom, the Lord told me to fast for three days with one meal a day."

My mom would say, "Okay, we're going to do that."

After the first day I would say, "Oh, my God, why did I tell her that I was going to do this?" She would see that I follow through with what I had said.

I thank God because it was my mother and father who led me in this direction.

I went to Ohio State University and while I was on campus, whenever anything would go wrong, I would call my mother. If I was sick or having a struggle I would call Mother and ask her to pray.

One day I was walking across campus; I was crying and I wanted to call Mother. The Lord spoke to me and said, "The One your mother goes to, you can go to. You don't have to go through your mother." And that was the start of my *real* dependence on God. I had depended on Him before then but it was a reality that had to click in somewhere. My mom had brought me to a certain point but I had to go a step further.

I really appreciate my mother and father because they lived a Christian life in front of me. I often tell people, "I wish my mom and dad had argued and fussed, then I would have known what real life is all about." I thought a home was supposed to be one of peace. We had fun because we had all the brothers and sisters we needed to play.

During my schooling there were things I needed and would ask God for. I realized that God is concerned about every phase of my life—even the clothes I wear. When I was thirteen years old I wanted a navy blue dress. I told my mother and she said, "Well, talk to God about it." I asked God for a navy blue dress. My aunt was what we called a "day-worker." That evening my aunt came home with a navy blue dress. It was gorgeous and was something that my family would not have been able to purchase for me. Those kinds of experiences encouraged me to have a relationship with God so I could ask and receive what I needed.

Wright

Apart from your parents, who are the other people who were influential in the development of your faith?

Petty

There was a Sunday school teacher, Mrs. Bethea. I used to say I wanted to be just like Sister Bethea. I was impressed with her because she had so many miracles that happened in her life. The way she talked and the experiences she had really made me believe that if God can do that for her He can do it for me.

Then there was my pastor, Bishop Samuel Hancock, in Detroit, Michigan. When I was seven years old we moved to Detroit from Louisville, Kentucky. Bishop Hancock made an impact on my life because he had only completed the fifth grade but this guy stood up against theologians and college professors. You would never believe that this man didn't have a doctorate in theology. It was because of his relationship with God. Some of the experiences he had in life were remarkable. He shared once about a time when he didn't have any food in his house. He got up that morning (it was in the wintertime) and he opened the door and there were groceries on his doorstep that someone had brought. He hadn't shared his need with anyone, however, God knew and supplied his need. He talked about how he traveled once from California to Detroit and had to pray that his tires wouldn't give out (they were bald).

Another influence in my faith walk is Gloria and Kenneth Copeland. Years ago, when they first started, they did a lot of faith teaching. One day I heard Gloria say that she had heard Oral Roberts say he had talked to Jesus and said, "I want to get to really know you, Jesus."

Jesus said to him, "Do you really want to get to know me?"

Oral Roberts said, "Yes."

Jesus said, "I want you to read Matthew, Mark, Luke, John, and Acts three times within thirty days."

Gloria said that when she heard that she wanted to do it too. She told her family that they would have to help her with her work around the house. When she started doing this she said she had more time—the family didn't have to help her do anything.

When I heard her testimony it seemed as though something grabbed me in the pit of my stomach and I thought I want to do that too. At that time I had a speaking engagement in Yakima, Washington. I said, "I'm going to do this and do it in fifteen days. I'm going to read Matthew, Mark, Luke, John, and Acts." The day I started, I was downtown in Seattle and I had a fastback Volkswagen. I reached in the back of my car to pick up my Bible to start reading (I was on my way to the beauty shop). When I backed out of the car, my foot got caught in the seatbelt and I fell headfirst on the concrete ground. Ironically, the only thing I was concerned about was whether I had gotten a run in my stockings. I didn't even consider the fact that I could have gotten a concussion or broken arm.

The exciting thing was that as I fell it was like something picked me up and I stood straight up. People asked me if I was hurt and I told them I wasn't—that I was fine. I closed the car door and went to my appointment. That was on a Friday. It wasn't until Saturday when I was showering that I saw a bruise on my left hip. I wondered what it was from and the thought came to me, "You really fell and the bruise is to show you that you were protected." That was a great experience for me because I got more done during that time when I was reading. It was like I was walking alongside Jesus as I was reading these chapters from the New Testament. It was such an exciting experience that I do it over and over again periodically because I get something new every time I do it.

In your faith lifestyle it's good to have partners. There are people in my life I've partnered with such as Dr. Willa Moore, and my sister, Dr. Addie Davis, Dr. June Hairston, and minister Jo Anne Hairston. I have a friend, Glynnis Ashley, who is another who has been very instrumental in my faith walk.

My faith partners share what God is doing in our lives—the miracles and the things we see and understand. Because of that it helps us grow and get stronger in our faith walk.

Wright

What are the things or practices, you recognize as having contributed the most to your faith journey?

Petty

I believe in being transformed and I believe you have to change from the inside out with the help of the Lord. This is what has helped me. The Scripture says that the children of darkness are wiser than the children of light so one of the things I do is I like to read about and examine what other people are doing even though they don't claim to be Christians (even some other religious beliefs) because I want to see what is behind what they have faith in. Believe it or not, it helps me because I think if they believe that without God how much more should I believe God.

Let me give an example of what I'm talking about. I believe in affirmations—speaking things the way I want them to be now. I went to Korea several years ago. While I was there my watch stopped working. I had watched somebody on television here in the States who was making forks bend and doing and all kinds of things. That Friday I had prayed and said, "That man on television didn't even give you credit nor is he even thinking about you and he was doing those things. I'm asking you to make my watch start working. I'm here in a foreign country and I need something I can hold on to." I had been praying all day, "Lord, make my watch start working." As I laid down the thought came to me, "Charlotte, I will make the watch start working next year, or next month?"

I thought, "Oh, you want me to be specific." So I said, "In the morning I'll wake up and I'll pray." I had taken my watch off and put it on the nightstand. The next morning I woke up and put my watch in my hand. I said, "Father, in the name of Jesus, I ask that my watch start working right now and work two months after I get back in the States. In Jesus' name, amen." I looked at the watch and the second hand started moving. That led me to believe and understand that God wants me to be specific. As I grow in my faith walk I need to be specific in what I ask for.

Those are the kinds of things that have helped me. It's like gaining a stronger faith. I noticed, when I was a kid, in one of my classes when the children made noise the teacher said, "Put your heads down." And there were times that I really wanted to talk to God—I just wanted to pray and I would say, "Lord, I would like to pray right now. Would you let the children be noisy?" And do you know what? The children would start making noise and the teacher would say, "Heads down!" I would think, "Wow! I'm on to something!"

Another thing that helped me was that when I was twelve years old I was teaching Sunday school. We were in a large church. We believe in faith healing. This little boy in my class had a stomachache. I thought, "I can't leave the rest of my students and go find a preacher to pray for him." So I asked the little boy, "Do you believe that Jesus can take your pain away?"

He said, "Yes."

"I'm going to ask Jesus to take the pain out of your stomach," I laid my hand on him and I just said a simple prayer. I didn't know a lot about what I was doing and to pray in the name of Jesus and all that. I just said, "Lord, please take the pain away from this little boy."

I asked him how he felt and he said, "The pain is gone."

I thought, "Wow! I'm on to something!"

That was an important experience in my faith walk.

Wright

What is the most challenging test in your life that faith equipped you for?

Petty

The most challenging experience I had in my life was in 1984. After having my annual physical, I received a phone call from a specialist. He told me I needed to come in to see him. I was sitting on the table in the examining room, waiting for him to come and examine me. He came in and said, "Did Liz tell you that you had cancer?" (Liz was my regular doctor.)

Water jumped out of my eyes. I wasn't crying—I saw the water just jump and fall on the doctor's coat in front of me. I was an administrator for the state and I had some interviews to do that evening. After he talked to me and we scheduled a time for me to come back in, I got off the table and I thought I ought to go home and cry my eyes out. The next thought that came to me was no, go back to work and act as if nothing had ever happened.

I believe that faith is not denying that something negative is happening but I believe faith helps you defy it. So I decided to go back to the office. I did the interviews and acted as if I hadn't received the news. I went home and phoned my parents and told them what had happened. They said they would pray. The one thing I said was, "Either God is for real or He is a liar. Other people have said He has healed them, then He is going to heal me."

I went to Seattle and got three different opinions in the process from three different doctors. The doctor at the University of Washington did a more thorough examination. He told me I had a uterine cancer that is the worst of its kind. He said, "You have three to five years to live and we don't know how many of those years you've used up already."

I said, "I'm really going to trust God."

It came to me to tell my friend, Glynnis Ashley, "I want you to go to a health food store and tell them what my problem is."

She came back and told me what to do—I had to change my whole way of living. I had to change the way I ate, and everything I did. One day I was crying because I had to stop eating sugar. I was crying saying, "Oh God, I have to give up sugar for the rest of my life!" (I really like sugar.) God said, "Don't worry about the rest of your life, do it now!"

That was in January of 1984. In April of 1984 I was at my sister's house in Seattle. I had just awakened and different people had been telling me, "Charlotte, you're healed, you're healed."

I prayed, "God, you don't have to speak to me through someone else, you can talk to me. I want to know for myself." That morning at my sister's I woke up and the first thing that came out of my mouth was, "I am healed!" The strange thing about all of this was I went to an iridologist in El Paso, Texas, after that point. She was also a nutritionist. She checked me out and she didn't see cancer, which made me feel better.

One of the things I did made a lot of enemies. People would say, "Charlotte I'm going to pray for you."

I would say, "No. Let me tell you how to pray and if you can't pray like this, don't pray at all. Thank God for my healing. Don't ask Him to heal me. He's doing that already."

People would say, "Charlotte, you should continue to ask God for healing."

"I believe that I can ask and it's happening," I would tell them. "Healing is a process."

In August I experienced severe hemorrhaging. I lived in Olympia and my sister lived in Seattle. I had gone to work that morning and because of cramping and hemorrhaging I went home. My staff phoned my sister and told her, "Charlotte is going to kill us but you'd better come see about your sister."

She phoned my doctor and my doctor said, "Go get her, she's probably dying. But I want you to stop at St. Peter's Hospital before you bring her to Seattle." (I didn't know any of this.) We stopped at the hospital and we were able to make it to Seattle. Thank God my sister wasn't crying or anything because the doctor had told her that I would probably die before I got to Seattle but to bring me anyway.

I got to the hospital. They were shocked. They prepared me for surgery (I refused chemotherapy and radiation). Finally, I think it was on August 5, I said to God, "Oh God, you've healed me of cancer, why am I having surgery?" Later I learned I had numerous fibroids and I was told that this is was what was causing the hemorrhaging. I went through surgery and the doctors came to visit and told me they didn't find any cancer. They said, "We saw a scar but there was no cancer." I had truly been healed. So that experience increased my faith. It was amazing.

My friends, Glynnis Ashley and Gloria Manago, spent time with my sister, Addie, and me in the hospital. They didn't allow me to stay there by myself.

After my healing, the staff at work said, "We're so glad you're healed. We won't have to eat that yucky stuff anymore." I ate "live" food—I didn't eat any cooked food. I would take some of it for them. They would pretend it was good. I had to drink wheat grass juice and freshly juiced vegetable juices. I would juice wheat grass and share it with them. They claimed it was good but it was the most horrible thing to me. Everybody supported me during that time.

I wouldn't let anyone tell me anything negative. For example, if someone would start talking negatively about Aunt so-and-so, I would say, "Hey, hold it!" because I didn't need to be around anything negative.

After I was cleansed it was also dangerous to be sterile so then I had to learn how to balance my food intake. That's my life now; I'm very health conscious. I'm not a vegetarian, however.

Wright

Through your faith experiences, have you been able to help others?

Petty

Yes. Because of my faith lifestyle, my job is to share my experiences and to actually act as a coach to others, giving them tools. I do a lot of counseling. One of the things I will do is give people assignments.

I had a staff member come to me once who said, "I can't pass a written test."

"That's the reason why you can't pass the test," I said. "It's because you say you can't pass it." I gave her an affirmation and said, "I want you to say, 'I can pass this test.'" I told her to say the affirmation three times a day and the next time she had to take the test I told her I wanted her to say it seven times in the morning, at noon, and before she went to bed at night. I told her she had to religiously follow the regimen and she did. She passed the test with flying colors.

When I have people who come to me and talk negative, I teach them how to change their language. My concern is for people to learn how to become the people that God intended for them to become. This means that God had a plan. You're already a winner because, of all the sperm that floated around the egg, the only one that penetrated that egg was the one that produced you. God said He knew you before you were formed in your mother's womb (Jeremiah 1:5).

There was a young man I was speaking to the other night who has come to know the Lord but he was on drugs before he came. He was sorry he had been caught taking drugs. He was weak at a point and went back. He told me he "messed up." I told him, "No. It was a learning experience. What you need to know is that now you have the power to say no. What you can't do is think of what's going to happen next year. You have to determine that yesterday ended last night and not carry last night over into today. So you're going to learn by what you did. You took drugs and now you feel guilty, right?" He said he did. I said, "That's the way the adversary treats you. He helps you do wrong and then he wants to put a guilt trip on you. We have to give up guilt. So now you have to say to the devil, 'Get the hell out of my life.' You have to talk to him. You're going to be working with other young people and you can help them much better than I can because of the experience you have. So don't feel you should go off and hide. It was an experience you're going to use to make you stronger." That young man left with a different attitude.

Wright

Do you believe embracing a faith lifestyle that is driven by faith has the same relevance today as it has in the past?

Petty

I strongly do. I think it has even more relevance today than in the past. Do you know why? Because of the different ages of civilization that we have gone through that I read about in I believe it was Stephen Covey's book. The first age he mentioned was the hunter and gatherer age, then we moved into the agricultural age, then into the industrial age, and now we're in the information and knowledge age.

He purports that we're moving into the wisdom age. In every century—in every progressing age—faith should be greater. Your faith lifestyle demands that you improve or be enhanced because of the things that happened and that are going to happen.

Wright

How has your faith helped you to succeed as a pastor who is female in a male influenced culture?

Petty

I strongly believe that as a child of God I am redeemed from the curse of the law and I'm a part of the body of Christ. I know that the Bible, which we in this day and age say that we believe in, has been translated from its original text. I'm so glad that I have a relationship with God and that I know, as a part of the family of God, He doesn't make a difference between His children. The reason we have done certain things is because of tradition rather than biblical principles.

One of the things I'm excited about is when I first started pastoring I went to a meeting in my denomination where they said that men would never belong to a church that a woman pastored. When we started the church I pastor, there were two men and three women (at least we had men). I came back home and we prayed and I said, "Lord, we want men to be attracted to You, I want men saved." At one time I had more men in my church than I had women.

One of the things I am concerned about is understanding. The Lord says He placed us in the body (the church) as it pleased Him. I had been prepared for this job in the secular world because I was an administrator with the state; at one time I was manager of the local office, which was the largest office in the state. I then rose to higher positions of management on up to an administrative post in our business office. What happened was that God prepared me as a leader. I was responsible for eliminating gender specific titles in job orders. We used to have the terms "waitress" and "waiters" but as we progress into the different centuries, *everyone* is now educated, everyone has skills and abilities. The Lord prepared me in the world of work. In the secular world God prepared me for leadership for the body of Christ and He placed me as a pastor of a congregation.

Wright

What a great conversation. Today we've been talking to The Reverend Dr. Charlotte B. Petty who is a pastor of a growing congregation. It is her conviction that we believe that which we do. She is a prominent Christian leader and, as we have found out today, is truly helping others.

Thank you so much, Dr. Petty, for being with us on *Speaking of Faith.*

About the Author

Charlotte B. Petty has over forty-five years of teaching and training experience both in the religious and secular arenas. She served as Director of Christian Education at Bethel Christian Church in Seattle for over twenty years. Her professional career in the secular arena consisted of managing the largest state employment office within the Washington State Employment Security Department, with a staff of over 500 people. As Deputy Assistant Commissioner, she was in charge of the Employer Tax Operation that included over 120,000 employers and funds of over $3 billion. Later she became the Assistant Commissioner of Employment Services for the entire State.

Retired from government she founded the Risen Faith Fellowship, a Cell Group Ministry Church in Olympia, Washington, in 1990, with five adults and two children. To date the church has grown to over 350 members and continues to grow.

As a member of the local Pacific Northwest District Council and national Pentecostal Assemblies of the World, Inc., religious organizations, she has been elevated to District Elder and Lay Director of the Western Region.

Charlotte B. Petty
Transformative Living
1322 105th Lane, SE
Olympia, WA 98501
Phone: 360.352.4726
E-mail: clepetty@ix.netcom.com

Chapter 13

IONA HALSEY

David Wright (Wright)

Today we're talking with minister, teacher, and missionary, Iona Halsey. Iona has spent the last fourteen years doing ministry through Evangelistic Messengers' Association (EMA). EMA was founded in 1933 and is now located in Huntingdon, Tennessee. Iona is also serving as Mission Director of Evangelistic Messengers' Association International (EMAI). EMAI is the international outreach of EMA, serving over one thousand indigenous ministers in more than fifty countries.

Iona, welcome to *Speaking of Faith*.

Iona Halsey (Halsey)

Thank you, David. It is exciting to be sharing with you about one of my favorite subjects, which is "faith."

Wright

I imagine that without faith and trust in the Lord it would be very difficult, perhaps, even impossible, to be on the mission field.

Halsey

This is especially true when I go where I know no one. New endeavors become even more challenging when the plans include my living alone for extended periods of time without first learning the language.

Wright

This definitely must stretch your faith.

Halsey

Yes, it does. And it demands that I continually walk close to God. Although I cannot think of anything I would rather do than be walking by faith. I believe there are things the Lord has allowed me to accomplish during these last few years that I could never have done without having complete faith and trust in Him. So I hope that by sharing some of the obstacles I have overcome and steps I have taken to strengthen my faith walk, it will encourage others to also step out in faith to fulfill the calling on their lives.

Wright

I am certain it will. But first, I would like you to share a little background information concerning your life prior to your becoming a minister. This may help others to better understand why you have chosen to spend this part of your life doing missionary work—particularly, if I might add, at your age.

Halsey

Let's begin by taking the mystery out of my age. I was born July 14, 1932. I am so blessed to still be actively involved in ministry and missions.

Wright

Yes, you are! When did you first become involved as a missionary?

Halsey

Since I have four children and seven grandchildren, it wasn't until five years after my husband died that I became a full-time missionary. Since then I have ministered in several countries around the world.

For the last three years I have been living in Nicaragua and ministering in their churches, especially to the children. During this past year, with a generous supply of the Lord's help, I established, and served as director of More Than Conquerors (MTC) Primary School in El Crucero, with ninety students attending. This year, MTC has over five hundred students.

Wright

Starting a school in a foreign country sounds both challenging and rewarding.

Halsey

Very much so. However, since attending school is not mandatory in Nicaragua, many of our students' parents can neither read nor write. This makes it even a greater challenge to motivate these children to study.

So when our ministry decided to build a school in El Crucero, I felt the Lord wanted me to encourage these children, just as I had encouraged my own children, to study and do the best they could with the minds God had given them.

We have good classrooms, a wonderful place to play, and very dedicated teachers. But since many of our children come from single parent homes with very low or no income, I believe the two most important ingredients we have lavished on these children are the Word of God and "lots and lots" of tender loving care.

Wright

Did it pay off?

Halsey

Bountifully! The final reports for the end of our school year revealed that our children were in second place scholastically in the El Crucero school district of forty schools! Our teachers told us that we had accomplished what they felt was almost impossible to do in the first year. But together we did it! More importantly, we are also planting the precious seed of God's Word in these children's hearts. I am trusting the Lord for a hundredfold harvest in this area.

Wright

Wonderful! It seems you enjoy working in another country. When and how did you decide that this was what you would like to do?

Halsey

I was about sixteen and that particular day I was at a Christian Youth Rally. We were singing, "Living for Jesus," when I saw myself dressed in white with a circle of dark-colored people around me. At the time I did not realize it was a vision of what God wanted me to do during my lifetime. I remember crying, and today, I still want to cry when I hear or sing that song.

That was in the forties when teaching and nursing were about the only two professions open to women. Since in my vision I was dressed in white, I concluded that nursing must be what the Lord wanted me to do.

Wright

When and how did you prepare for the mission field?

Halsey

My dad promised me that when I finished high school, I could go to any school of my choice. Because of what I felt the Lord wanted me to do, I definitely wanted to go to a Christian school. With this in mind, I made my first choice. My dad said, "No, it is too far away."

My second choice was a Christian nursing school. This time the school doctor felt my dry skin might hinder me from completing the surgical training necessary to graduate, so I was not accepted.

My third choice was another Christian college. Again, and very emphatically, my father said, "No!" He knew two graduates from that collage who were not walking their talk. So I could not go there.

Wright

That must have been very discouraging. What was your next move?

Halsey

Our pastor, a former missionary, tried to persuade my father to change his mind. It was not a quiet discussion! My pastor even offered financial aid from the church because of my involvement in church activities. There was no changing my father's mind. I was devastated. It seemed like my open door of opportunity had just slammed shut before my very eyes.

Wright

Couldn't you have gotten a job and worked your way through school?

Halsey

Remember, this was in 1950. My older brother drove, so I never had the opportunity to learn to drive. I had never worked away from home, or been away from my parents more than a week at Bible camp. To sum it up, I really knew nothing about the outside world.

Wright

What did you finally do? Did you go to school somewhere else?

Halsey

Yes, I went to a secular school of nursing. But a certain ingredient was missing. I did not know exactly what it was or what was happening to me. But having just recovered from a serious blood condition, I felt physically drained and mentally discouraged and defeated. It was the beginning of my downhill slide into a world of nightmares, depression and despair.

Wright

Let's see, you were about eighteen years old at that time. Couldn't you have discussed these problems with your parents or your friends?

Halsey

Had this been allowed, I probably would have learned that 99 percent of my disturbing thoughts were just part of growing up. However, one of my mother's favorite sayings was, "What will people think?" This kept me quiet about my feelings, fears, and frustrations. Instead, these negative feelings were kept bottled up inside me to fester, multiply, and manifest themselves through horrible nightmares.

Wright

I certainly can see where not feeling free to share your thoughts and apprehensions with others could cause serious problems. What happened next?

Halsey

I wish I could tell you my troubles were over. I wish I could tell you I had learned to trust the Lord in such a great and wonderful way that I was walking with Him by faith. But none of these things were true, not yet anyway.

In 1960, three months after my fourth child was born, I was hospitalized for four months in a mental institution. I never attempted suicide, but just in case the walls of my mind closed in on me too tightly, I always had to have a plan of escape. Even while I was in the hospital, I had a plan. Yet, what kept me from taking my own life was that I believed, and still do, that suicide is murder. Very often I have felt that life here on earth was a living hell; this made me even more determined not to spend my eternity in hell. This thought kept me alive until God's truth got through to me.

Wright

Were you able to get help when you were in the hospital?

Halsey

It would have been worth it, if being hospitalized had been the answer; but it only made things worse. Now I had to live with the stigmatism of having been in a mental hospital. Whenever someone learned that I had been institutionalized, it seemed our relationship changed. It definitely changed my relationship with my neighbors. No longer did they leave their children in my care when they needed to go on an errand uptown.

Wright

So how did you cope?

Halsey

With tranquilizers! For most of twenty-six years, tranquilizers were definitely a part of my life—nothing to be proud of, but they kept me going. By then I was fully convinced I had a mental problem and only tranquilizers could ease my thoughts and take the edge off my depression.

Wright

Did you live in a constant state of despair and depression?

Halsey

No, there were good days too. I worked and was successful at what I was doing. I raised my children and they did very well in school.

Yet, I was living my life depending on pills. Doesn't make sense, does it?

Wright

No! It doesn't make sense at all! But tell me more about your depression. What was it like and how did you feel?

Halsey

I called it a black depression. It was like a black cloud hanging over my head and closing in around me. It even felt black. And that is where I was so often. At those times I wanted to die. Yet, I knew I must not take my own life. I begged God to please erase all the depressing thoughts in my mind. It seemed that even my prayers could not penetrate this black cloud above me. They would only bounce back at me until finally, the cloud would lift once again.

Wright

Did you feel guilty about being so depressed?

Halsey

Yes, I certainly did. I could not help but wonder about what great wrong I may have done. But those who are depressed today can be encouraged by God's Word as we read in 2 Corinthians 1:8, that even our great Apostle Paul—a man of great faith and a great writer of many of the New Testament books—tells us how he " . . . despaired even of life."

Even though we may feel that God has forsaken us, we must take heart that depression happened, and still happens, even to God's most faithful servants. In 1 Kings 19:4, Elijah " . . . sat down under a juniper tree and he requested for himself that he might die; when he said, 'It is enough; now, O Lord, take away my life; for I am not better than my fathers.' "

Wright

Do you feel there are many today who are experiencing similar problems?

Halsey

Oh! Yes, I do. This is why I am sharing this part of my life with you, and putting it on the printed page. I know there are many in this world, and just as many in our churches, who are crying out for release from the prison of their minds, their thoughts and emotions, their present situations, or their tainted pasts. They are in a mental prison and they are looking for the key.

Wright
But you must have found your way through the maze or you wouldn't be on the mission field today.

Halsey
Eventually I did! I was constantly seeking but could not find the answer. Physically and mentally I was walking a tight rope. I was smoking over a pack of cigarettes a day, drinking too much coffee, taking pills to cope, and pills to sleep, hoping I could sleep without having nightmares.

Wright
How were you doing physically?

Halsey
Again, in 1979, I began having serious health problems. First it was mononucleosis. Then major surgery. If the doctors were suspecting cancer, they found none. In 1980 I had another major surgery—again no cancer.

Wright
It sounds like you needed a mental, physical, *and* spiritual miracle.

Halsey
Yes. I did. But the Lord did get my attention during this time. Deep inside I knew I must make my walk with Him the priority of my life, or my next surgery would be for cancer. His warning left no doubt in my mind that all roads lead to death and hell except the one found in Matthew 7:14, " . . . strait is the gate, and narrow is the way, which leadeth unto life, and few there be that find it." I had to find the way. I felt that hell must be real! I thought I was living it!

Wright
What do you believe is the cause and answer for mental problems?

Halsey

I believe our answer is found in John 10:10 where it tells us that Satan is the cause. He comes to steal our joy, kill our spirit, and destroy our soul. How can we be all that God has called us to be when we are bound up in our problems and emotions? How can we reach out and help others?

Who is our answer? Jesus is our only answer. But once Satan has his clutches on us, he will not give us up easily. I learned that getting from Satan to Jesus can be a very painful and tedious journey.

Wright

How did you get from Satan to Jesus?

Halsey

I had tried many things, "*plus* God," with little or no success. But I had never tried "*only* God!" God arranged for Jeremiah to get "out of his horrible pit," surely He could do the same for me.

Wright

What do you mean when you say, "getting out of your horrible pit?"

Halsey

First, let me share with you about Jeremiah's pit found in Jeremiah 38:6–13. Jeremiah's enemies had thrown him into a pit. There was no water in this pit, but there was a *lot* of mud. So much mud that Jeremiah sank in it.

One of the king's servants heard about Jeremiah's predicament and went to the king to beg for permission to free Jeremiah out of his pit before he died from hunger. The king not only granted the servant's request, but sent along thirty men just in case the enemy showed up to cause trouble and try to hinder the rescue. All went well and Jeremiah got out of his pit.

Wright

How does this relate to *your* pit?

Halsey

Like Jeremiah, there was a time when I felt I was lying face down in a deep muddy pit. People were walking on me, trying to force my face even deeper into the mud. But I could go no lower because there was a concrete floor under the mud; yet they kept on walking on me. I had reached the bottom of my despair, but my enemies still were not satisfied.

At that time of my life, I desperately needed the loving arms of my Savior to reach down and pull me out of my miry pit and free me from the many enemies that were surrounding me.

Wright

That must have been a very difficult time. But you look so healthy today, I can only conclude that you overcame all your destructive habits.

Halsey

Yes, eventually I did, but like Jeremiah I needed to be rescued. I needed the King of kings to come personally and help me out of my miry clay.

In John 8:32 Jesus promises us, "Ye shall know the truth, and the truth shall make you free." Thank goodness He doesn't open a door and *"set"* us free just as we are—miserable, depressed, discouraged and ready to give up.

No! Jesus *makes* us free by molding, shaping, and changing us from the inside out. It was time for me to submit to Jesus, so He could "make" me free according to John 8:36, "If the Son therefore shall make you free, ye shall be free indeed" (KJV). I desperately wanted to be free in Jesus.

Wright

You are right! Most people do say "set," but it reads "make" free. Quite a difference! So when and how did you begin to get out of your horrible pit?

Halsey

Here's where faith steps in because, " . . . without faith it is impossible to please him: for he that cometh to God must believe that He is, and that He is a rewarder of them that diligently seek Him."— Hebrews 11:6

Wright

With all of your problems, where did you start?

Halsey

I started with myself. Believe me, it takes faith to conquer self. But one day I looked into my mirror and said, "From now on, Iona, no one is to blame for your mistakes, but you."

Adam introduced the bad habit of "blaming others" in the Garden of Eden after he had eaten the forbidden fruit. First he blamed God. Next he blamed Eve. Then Eve blamed the snake. Neither accepted their blame. Apparently they both forgot—they could have said, "No!" to the fruit.

Wright

You're right. When we make a mistake, it is so easy to blame others.

Halsey.

It takes faith to admit we are wrong and trust God for whatever consequences may follow. Whom do we think we are fooling anyway? Let's face it! Nothing is hid from God, " . . . thou knowest my foolishness; and my sins are not hid from thee" (Psalm 69:5). Deciding to accept responsibility for my mistakes was the beginning of my getting out of my horrible pit.

Wright

Which habit was the first to go?

Halsey

Because the inevitable happened, tranquilizers were the first to go. I had been taking several tranquilizers during the day, then a sleeping pill at night. One morning I did not, and could not, wake up. It was three in the afternoon before I could begin to even focus. That's when fear set in. I realized that the next time I might not wake up. But how could I make it without my pills?

By faith, I disposed of every pill. Even though I had been taking tranquilizers for almost twenty-six years, and as impossible as it may seem, I do not remember having any withdrawal symptoms. That was in 1979. Since then I have never taken another tranquilizer. I am free! God is so good!

Wright

I am certain there are people reading this who, like you, would like to be free from depending upon tranquilizers. But isn't it dangerous to quit "cold turkey" as you did? Shouldn't it be done under a doctor's supervision?

Halsey

You are right in both of your statements. It can be dangerous to suddenly quit a medication of such long duration without the supervision of a doctor. I do not recommend it. But in my ignorance and desperation, I believe God blessed me with a miracle or I would not be here to tell you about it.

In 1979 I believe Jesus did another miracle in my life. I was listening to a Bible teacher who was comparing our minds to computers. He was explaining how everything that happens to us—good or bad—is stored in our memories. With all the bad thoughts, worries, and problems I had stored up in my mind, no wonder I was having nightmares and difficulty sleeping.

Wright

Did the teacher tell you how you could stop these negative thoughts?

Halsey

I do not know because at that moment something came to my mind that would change my life forever. I remembered how Jesus used God's Word to defeat the devil in the wilderness. Since Jesus is our example, everything He did we can also do if only we have faith. So I decided that for every negative thought in my mind, I was willing to listen and replace it with two positive thoughts. From then on, that was exactly what I did. Day and night I filled my mind with the Word of God, Christian music, and Bible teaching tapes. With a steady diet of God's Word I was hoping to drive out every negative thought.

Wright

What were you building your faith on?

Halsey

On Romans 10:17, "Faith cometh by hearing, and hearing by the word of God." Sometimes whole verses, other times, only a word or two would come into my mind or spirit. Even at night God would wake me with the Word. My part was to get out of bed and search the Bible because God had a message, a word of warning, encouragement, or an answer for me.

Philippians 4:8 tells us that it is very important to God what we think about, "Finally, brethren, whatsoever things are true, whatsoever things are honest, whatsoever things are just, whatsoever things are pure, whatsoever things are lovely, whatsoever things are of good report; if there be any virtue, and if there be any praise, think on these things."

Wright

Were you finally able to sleep peacefully?

Halsey

There were still times I would worry about trivial things I could do nothing about, but finally I took to heart Matthew 6:33, " Seek ye first the kingdom of God, and His righteousness; and all these things shall be added unto you." As I was earnestly seeking the kingdom of God and His integrity and purity in my thinking, feeling, and acting, I read the Bible through in only nine months. When we seek Him first, He promises to take care of "all these things." All of what things? Our food, drink, clothing, and other necessities. Pretty simple, isn't it?

Wright

Faith seems so simple. Do you think we make it too difficult?

Halsey

Perhaps, but slowly my mountain was beginning to crumble and I was sleeping all night. No more bad dreams. What a victory! As it says in Psalm 4:8, "I will both lay me down in peace, and sleep: for thou, Lord, only makest me dwell in safety."

Now I'm teaching our school children that if they will always keep God first, He will take care of their needs. That's what His Word promises!

Wright

Now how about your health? You're looking well. Does that mean you have overcome your health problems too?

Halsey

Thank you! I am enjoying good health today. As you know, this wasn't always true. One day when I was walking, I became so exhausted I began complaining to the Lord. I asked, "Aren't I ever going to feel well again?"

God's answer was simple and to the point. "You did not get this way in one day." And I knew what He was talking about.

Wright
What was He talking about?

Halsey
My bad habits. There were still some personal habits I needed to conquer. Yes, God could have healed me instantly, but unless I changed my habits I would only be back again in the same shape very soon. I had work to do before I could claim Isaiah 58:8, "Then shall thy light break forth as the morning, and thine health shall spring forth speedily."

Wright
What was the first bad habit you overcame?

Halsey
Coffee! But this was quite easy to overcome because one night my heart began to palpitate so fast I could not move! Medically, they say this can cause a stroke. I began praying that if God would keep me alive, I promised never to touch coffee again. Well! I'm still alive and I have kept my word.

Wright
Many people may not feel that coffee is so bad for their health.

Halsey
Perhaps not for them, but for me it definitely was and I knew I must quit. The same was true of cigarettes! How could I ask God to keep me healthy if I continued smoking? It was a slow suicide. But the most important reason was that as a Christian, if I could not conquer my bad habits, how could I help others to overcome their habits of drugs, alcohol, etc.?

I chose my fiftieth birthday as my day to quit. But unlike quitting my tranquilizers, this time I suffered. The first three days were almost unbearable! I begged the Lord to please help me. There was no instant freedom from the habit. Instead, He armed me with His Word, "Commit thy way unto the Lord; trust also in him; and he shall bring it to pass."—Psalm 37:5

Wright

How did this Scripture help you overcome cigarettes?

Halsey

I felt the Lord was saying, "Commit this cigarette unto me, trust me, and I will bring it to pass." Whenever I had the desire to smoke, I would quote Psalm 37:5 and the urge would leave. For two weeks I did not smoke. Then I cheated and smoked a few cigarettes. But the next day I started another two smoke-free weeks. Again, for one day I smoked. Strange as it was, this seemed to be the pattern of my quitting.

At that time we were living in the Ozarks in Missouri. So every day I was walking for several miles in the fresh air, trying to breathe deeply to cleanse my lungs of thirty years of smoking. With every two-week period of not smoking, my body was slowly adjusting to doing without nicotine. Then the day came when I smoked only one cigarette and got so sick I was rolling on my bed. But I was praying, "Please Lord, keep me sick until I never want another one." He did, and I have not touched a cigarette since.

Wright

Sounds like a tough battle. Was it worth it?

Halsey

Oh my, yes! God knew the best way for me to quit so I would never return to the habit. And it worked! That was twenty-three years ago. God tells us to resist the devil and he will go. And fast! "Submit yourselves therefore to God. Resist the devil, and he will flee from you" (James 4:7). God made me free, and I am free indeed!

Wright

Were there any other areas in your life that God pinpointed for a change?

Halsey

Fear! I was fearful of going to sleep because of nightmares. Fearful of heights. Fearful of being shut in. Fearful of swimming after I nearly drowned. Fearful of "what others might think." Fearful of failure. Fearful of living. Fearful of dying. But 2 Timothy 1:7 tells us that, "God hath not given us the spirit of fear." This leaves Satan as the source of our fears. But we can overcome Satan with God's Word

" . . . because greater is He that is in you, than He that is in the world."—1 John 4:4

Wright

These are all very good. What else do we need faith to overcome?

Halsey

Compromising! It seems to have become a way of life, even for Christians. No longer is a lie called a lie. Instead, we say they did not speak the truth. But God says in Revelation 21:8, " . . . all liars, shall have their part in the lake which burneth with fire and brimstone." Very clear, isn't it?

Concerning abortions, I used to say, "It is your decision, but I would never have an abortion." One day my thoughts were something like this, "Abortion is murder. So really abortion is wrong, unless perhaps, in cases of incest or rape." God interrupted my thoughts with these words, "Don't you think I can take care those who are pregnant because of rape and incest too?" I immediately repented saying, "Lord, forgive me, murder is murder; whether the baby is the result of rape, incest, or by consent." I did not realize how compromising my thinking had become until I read Revelation 3:16, "So then because thou art lukewarm, and neither cold nor hot, I will spue thee out of my mouth." God will not tolerate us being lukewarm, compromising, making excuses, or excusing others for doing things He clearly calls sin. "Yet ye say, The way of the Lord is not equal . . . Is not my way equal? are not your ways unequal?"—Ezekiel 18:25

Wright

So we are either on God's side or Satan's side. Is that true?

Halsey

It is our choice! But if we choose to disobey God's Word, we will pay! "For without are dogs, and sorcerers, and whoremongers, and murderers, and idolaters, and whosoever loveth and maketh a lie"— Revelation 22:15

Knowing the Lord never changes brought stability into my life. "For I am the Lord, I change not"—Malachi 3:6. Psalm 40:2 tells me He " . . . set my feet upon a rock, and established my goings." The Rock that never changes—"Jesus Christ the same yesterday, and to day, and for ever" (Hebrews 13:8)—the solid Rock! "I shall not be greatly moved."—Psalm 62:2

Wright

I like that. It takes faith to stand firm when everything is against you.

Halsey

Yes, it does—like my being in a mental institution became an albatross around my neck. There were those who used this knowledge to manipulate, control, and blame me whenever something went wrong. I was their scapegoat. They would say, "You will always have a problem coping." "The doctors say you will never get well." "Are you taking your pills? If you were, we wouldn't be having this problem, etc." It is true, "Faith comes by hearing." And the same is true of negative reports. The more we hear them, the sooner we believe them.

However, in 1978 a certain accusation caused me to retrieve my medical report to learn about my prognosis when I was hospitalized in 1960. What I learned awed me! My doctor's report said nothing about my being mentally ill. It only said I was under tremendous stress and because of this stress, my life was in danger. For more than eighteen years I was led to believe I had a mental problem. And then, thousands of pills later, I was to learn I was a victim of stress and verbal abuse. How I survived and was able to function mentally after taking all those tranquilizers, only God knows.

God's says in 2 Timothy 1:7 that He has given us "a sound mind." When God says He has given me a sound mind, by faith I can claim a sound mind.

Wright

It must have been shocking news to learn you were never mentally ill. What was your next step?

Halsey

Faith to forgive. God cannot forgive us until we forgive others. Even when we have done nothing to deserve the offense, we must still leave it in God's hands. He promises, "Vengeance is mine; I will repay" (Deuteronomy 32:35 and Romans 12:19). Healing comes to our minds and spirits when we forgive others.

And God is ready and waiting to forgive us of our sins, but we must ask. When we repent, we must believe and receive by faith that the blood of Jesus is powerful enough to wash us free from *all* sin.

Then " . . . as far as the east is from the west, so far hath he removed our transgressions from us."—Psalm 103:12

Wright
Now were you ready for your future?

Halsey
Yes, now I had faith to face the future. Once I began hearing and knowing God's voice, I learned that He has a lot to say about everything we do, if we will only listen. When my husband died I was fifty-three years old. The desire to make the rest of my time here on earth count began to occupy my thoughts. But the questions were: what to do and where to begin? Then the thought of ministry came to my mind and this conversation took place, "Lord, I am getting too old for that." The Lord said, "So was Moses." I thought about that and realized it was true. Moses was eighty years old before he was called to do a great work for God. So my next protest was, "But I am a woman." God replied, "With me nothing is impossible." What more could I say? From then on, ministry was on my mind.

Wright
As I remember, you were first called by the Lord to the mission field when you were sixteen. Did this become a reality?

Halsey.
Yes, it did. On the first of October 1991, I joined Evangelistic Messengers' Association then located in Cleveland, Tennessee, as a volunteer.

- In 1993 I crossed the Atlantic Ocean to Nigeria for my first mission trip.
- 1993–1996 was spent founding and teaching our More Than Winners Bible School in Uzgorod, Ukraine.
- January 17, 2003, I went to El Crucero, Nicaragua to help build and establish More Than Conquerors Primary School.
- What's next? Only the Lord knows!

Wright
Thank you, Iona for your encouraging words.

Today we have been talking with Iona Halsey. Through her testimony about the many obstacles she has had to overcome in her life, I hope she has encouraged and taught many of you readers how you can also be "overcomers."

Iona, would you please summarize the seven steps you believe are the most important for us if we desire to continually walk by faith?

Halsey

I'll be glad to share with you my "Seven Steps To Becoming An Overcomer—No Matter What Comes Against You:"

1. I believe we must assume responsibility for our own mistakes and stop trying to find reasons to blame our parents, our past, or others for our mistakes.
2. We must be totally reliant on the Lord and His Word.
3. We must forgive others so we can receive God's forgiveness.
4. We must not limit God by how old we are or what our present circumstances may be. When God calls us into His service, no matter how many obstacles may come our way, we must persevere. He proved this to me when I finally became a missionary forty-four years after I first felt His calling.
5. We must make ourselves available to God by purposing to "invest" our lives and not just "spend" them.
6. We must be willing to allow God to stretch our faith so the impossible becomes the possible.
7. We must be willing to do whatever the Lord asks, when He asks, and go where He directs. It does not matter what others may think—what matters is what God says.

David, I believe that after we have taken these seven steps, one day we will be able to look back on our lives and say, "Look what the Lord has done. And to God be the glory. Amen!"

About the Author

IONA HALSEY began her life of serving others as an LPN working in hospitals located in Rochester, Minnesota, the home of the Mayo Clinic. People come from all over the world to this famous medical center with the hope of having their health restored. This was Iona's opportunity to meet and minister to their physical needs. After eighteen years in the medical field, Iona changed courses and became involved in sales. Again the world came to her for needs and gifts to take to their homes wherever that may be.

After her husband died in 1986, Iona's greatest desire was to invest her time helping others rather than just spending it. She became an ordained minister in 1989 through Evangelistic Messenger's Association located in Huntingdon, Tennessee. In 1991 she moved to the ministry center as a volunteer. At the age of sixty, she crossed the Atlantic waters to Nigeria for her first missionary trip. She then moved to the Ukraine where she lived for more than two years and established a More Than Winners School of Theology. She traveled on to minister in Hungary, Bulgaria, Romania, China, South Africa, Lesotho, Israel and more. No longer is the world coming to her—she is going to the world. The last three years she has been in Nicaragua where, in 2005, she established More Than Conquerors Primary School under New Hope Children's Foundation. MTC offers free education to children who otherwise are too poor to attend school. They also have the opportunity to study English and the Bible. MTC's first year was a great success, ranking scholastically number two among forty other primary schools in the same area—something almost impossible to obtain during the first year.

This year, as Director of Missions for EMAI, she will be traveling overseas to support and encourage EMAI indigenous ministers in a number of countries. Iona's desire is to give. In return she has received many blessings of victories; but most importantly, many, many wonderful friends all over the world.

Iona Halsey
100 Mission Lane
Huntingdon, TN 38344
E-mail: ionahalsey@gmail.com

Chapter 14

DAVE DRAVECKY

David E. Wright (Wright)

Today we are talking with Dave Dravecky. Dave was first rushed into the public spotlight in the late 1980s when his career took off as a major league baseball pitcher—a southpaw—for the San Francisco Giants.

Shortly after realizing his lifelong dream, Dave was diagnosed with a soft-tissue cancer in the deltoid muscle of his pitching arm. The next year was a whirlwind of surgery, radiation, pain, and depression all in the glaring light of the media. Eventually, Dave's arm was amputated to stop the spread of cancer and save his life.

Through it all, Dave's faith in God and love He gave him through others provided the anchor needed in the midst of the storm. Dave founded the Outreach of Hope in 1991 in response to the thousands of letters and requests he received from hurting people encouraged by his faith.

Dave, welcome to *Speaking of Faith.*

David Dravecky (Dravecky)
Thank you. It's a pleasure to talk with you today.

Wright
Tell us a little bit about your background—personally and professionally, if you will.

Dravecky
Well, actually I guess it revolves so much around the game of baseball—combining both the personal and professional side. You know, I was a little kid growing up with a dream, hoping that dream someday would become a reality. That dream was to be a major league pitcher—as a young boy that was a big part of my life. My summers were spent playing baseball and traveling around with Mom and Dad hauling me from one game to the next. It was a great life.

When I look back on those days as a kid, I am so grateful that my dad and mom were so supportive and encouraging. They didn't try to live their dream through me—that was a wonderful gift. They really did help to nurture that love for baseball I had, because of their attitude towards the game; they just wanted to see me do my best and have fun. As I progressed, obviously, things improved and my skills and talents developed to the point where I was able to go on to college baseball. I was drafted after four years at Youngstown State University where I played baseball.

The Pittsburgh Pirates drafted me in the twenty-first round and my professional baseball career began. I played for three seasons with the Pirates then in 1982 I received a phone call—I was being called up to the big leagues. I was traded over to the San Diego Padres in their minor league system. So that was a real exciting time in my life, obviously.

I was married at the time. My wife, Jan, and I had just had our first child. Tiffany was born and all of a sudden I'm hearing the news that I'm a big leaguer. So it was a very special time for us—becoming parents and being a part of the major leagues.

Then my career began as a major league baseball player from that point forward. I played with the Padres for almost five years. I had a wonderful time in that organization. It was awesome living in San Diego and playing baseball there. I was in an All Star game in 1983, the World Series in 1984, and then got traded in 1987 from the Padres, who at the time were in last place, to the first place San

Francisco Giants. That was a new beginning for my career, so to speak—being with the first place Giants. That year in '87 we went into the playoffs against the Cardinals, and we were in the championship game of the National League. Unfortunately, we didn't get to World Series that year, but it was a great year for me in the second half of the season; I was really looking forward to 1988 being my year. I was hoping to be a twenty-game winner for the first time and things were really starting to come together.

In 1988 I opened up for the Giants against the Dodgers; we defeated them five to one. Things were really going my way. I was kicking it off the right way. By September of '88, along with arm problems that I had had during the summer, a small lump had developed to half the size of a golf ball on my left arm. In September of that year, the doctors diagnosed cancer in my left arm and I had to go in and remove the tumor along with 50 percent of my deltoid muscle.

Needless to say, that was a very difficult time in our lives, and we were very grateful for our faith in Jesus Christ. During that time, we were really relying on God's strength to endure the journey we were facing. The doctor said that outside of a miracle, I would never pitch again. Ten months later, I was standing on the mound in Candlestick Park getting ready to throw the first pitch against the Cincinnati Reds! So it was a very special time—an incredible moment too hard to put into words. I guess if there's one thing I can say, it was an awesome experience to see God grant me another opportunity, along with all those wonderful people who helped me to get there—the doctors, the nurses, the therapists, the trainers—all the people who put forth the effort to help me get physically strong enough to be able to throw a baseball again.

Wright
Does the deltoid muscle actually grow back?

Dravecky
No, it does not. So I was literally pitching without a deltoid muscle because the doctors had told me that when they remove 50 percent of the muscle, in essence 95 percent of the use of it is lost. So therapy was critical to developing other muscles and tendons and things in that area to compensate for the strength the deltoid muscle provided to be able to throw a baseball. That first day back was a real special day in view of all those facts and knowing that the doctor had said outside of a miracle I'd never pitch. To actually go out and pitch was

just an incredible experience. We won that day four to three. I pitched eight innings, got the win, and we defeated the Cincinnati Reds.

Needless to say, I was really feeling good about where my career was headed now and that the cancer was behind me—they had taken it out. I thought that it was gone for good, and so I proceeded to focus on my baseball career once again. Five days later we were in Montreal. I was pitching against the Expos and pitching extremely well. I was back in the groove. Then in the sixth inning I went out and threw a fastball and my left arm snapped in half. As a result, my career came to an end.

The doctors examined the arm and there was more cancer. They had to go in and do more surgeries and subsequent radiation therapy. I ended up with a staph infection for ten months. Over a two-year period it was a difficult struggle battling with not only the physical side of it, but also with the emotional and the spiritual side of the journey—wondering if God really cared.

I was going through clinical depression, fighting all those issues that we fight when we're facing cancer and it doesn't seem to go away—facing my own mortality, fear of dying, doubts about where God is, frustration over the pain, and just the lack of being able to do things I really enjoy. Most importantly, for me, I had to face not being able to play baseball any more just when I was at the prime of my career.

It all culminated on June 18, 1991, when the doctors went in to remove my left arm and shoulder for fear that the cancer would spread to the main part of my body. That's when, along with all the other things I had been facing, the clinical depression intensified and I basically went through an identity crisis. If I could no longer play baseball, then who is this guy and what can I do with my life?

That was a very difficult period of time for me but God was so faithful to bring people into the picture to encourage us—to encourage me—to reveal His love and His faithfulness to us. As we experienced all those things, not only from friends and family, but also through counseling, we began to heal. A lot of that healing took place as a result of just being honest about our pain and taking the necessary steps to get that stuff out and to start dealing with it, and realizing that there is more to life than just baseball. That was a huge step for us, and we've been on that journey ever since.

Wright

Can you tell our readers a little bit about Outreach of Hope and how that all came about?

Dravecky

Well, I think a big part of it was that because of the platform I had in major league baseball so many people were aware of my story. The public exposure was huge. I mean everybody was following this kid who was diagnosed with cancer and made a comeback, and then broke his arm in a game after the comeback five days later. So it was big news all over the nation.

As a result, because of my struggles, people began to share their stories with us by sending us mail and telling us what they were struggling with. Obviously, my wife is a people-pleaser, and as a result felt the weight of those letters that came in and felt the need to respond to all of them. There were tens of thousands of pieces of mail that came to our home. I mean, I couldn't park my car in my garage simply because the mail took up all the space. As a result, we made the effort to try and respond to these people—to be a source of encouragement to them in the same way that people had encouraged us on our journey. That's really how it all began. It began as a result of our desire to want to help others in the same way that we had been helped, and to really come alongside people and let them know just how much God really does care for them on the journey.

For some people, as Christians, encouragement was the reality that God is faithful to walk with them through that valley in life. For others who were questioning God—who maybe were seeking God— and all of a sudden tragedy came into their life, it was an opportunity to introduce them to the One who offers hope.

So over the last eleven years, through the Outreach of Hope, we've had the privilege of being able to encourage people who not only battle with cancer or amputation, but who are just hurting out there and need encouragement from someone. It's been a real privilege to come alongside those people.

You know, Jan and I often say that God took away our strength. For her it was her battle with clinical depression—she relied so much on her mind. She was very strong mentally (not to say that she isn't now). For me my strength was my arm. As a result of those experiences—her going through the depression and me losing my arm—we became obviously much more dependent on God and trusted Him more. With that, our desire then became being able to reach out and encourage others in this same way that we had been encouraged by Him—applying the whole concept of comforting others in the same way we had been comforted.

Wright

Having grown up in a Christian home and being raised with those kinds of beliefs, I can't help entertaining the thought at least—even though I am convinced that God does not create or cause cancer—since God chooses people to do His work, one thing was taken away from you in order for you do a greater thing.

Dravecky

Oh, there's no question in my mind when I look at this that baseball was just a stepping-stone to something greater. It took a few years to discover what that was because before we were able to actually respond the way we've responded through the Outreach of Hope over all these years, we had to first go through the fire—we had to go through the refining process. I am convinced that there were things in our lives we had to deal with. Pride was one of them. When you're in a sport that is exposed nationally, then you're in the public limelight, you're treated almost as if you were a god. You can't help but allow that to affect you.

Wright

Not to mention the financial reward of playing in the big leagues.

Dravecky

Exactly. There were a lot of issues both of us had to deal with in those areas. There were things in our lives, and there was baggage we carried that we had to deal with. God allowed us to go through that refining process for a very important reason, and that was to bring us up out of those things.

Ron Lee Davis, the pastor I got to know several years ago, wrote a book called *Gold in the Making*. The subtitle was *Affliction Is Gold in the Making*. What we've come to realize is that going through that purification process was to allow us to become a more pure form of precious metal in God's eyes. Quite frankly, the fact is we'll probably be refined several times more because that's the journey of life—the sanctification process. It's been a really special thing for us to experience.

Wright

My wife is a cancer survivor of several years now, and there was a time when it was very, very questionable whether or not she was going to make it. I was in a meeting with her some time ago and she told the group that even though she doesn't want to go through cancer again—and all it implies for both her and the entire family—she wouldn't give a million dollars for the experience. I've heard a lot of cancer survivors say that same thing. Of course, it confuses people like me.

Dravecky

There's no question in my mind that cancer has been a blessing in my life. There was a point where I couldn't say that; but I've gotten to the other side now. I've seen the benefits of that experience in my own life. It's changed Jan and me both to the point that we now do what we do through the Outreach of Hope. It really has created in us a desire to bring encouragement in the lives of others, to really introduce them to God's love through His Son, Jesus Christ, letting them know not only that we care, but more importantly, God cares about them on their journey.

Wright

So what is the mission for Outreach of Hope?

Dravecky

The mission is basically to serve suffering people, especially people battling with cancer and amputation. We offer resources for encouragement, comfort, and hope through a personal relationship with Jesus Christ. That is the real mission of the Outreach of Hope. We're here to offer resources to folks, and those resources are really designed to provide encouragement, comfort, and hope through Jesus Christ as they face their battle.

We publish a magazine called *The Encourager* that we send out at no cost to all the families who are referred to the ministry. Those who support our ministry are recipients of *The Encourager* magazine as well. The magazine deals with all the issues we've struggled with over the years as we've gone through the battle with cancer, and what comes afterward. It's been a real privilege to be a part of what God has allowed us to do throughout these past eleven years through the Outreach of Hope. It's been a very special journey.

Wright

Do you do any public speaking, hold workshops, or have seminars to help people?

Dravecky

We have, from time to time, participated in cancer support groups to encourage them in relationship to the encouragement they offer to people who would also participate in those groups. There are times when Jan and I have gone out and actually spoken in churches and in other venues about the work we do. But because of the limitations we have financially, we don't actually see that as a part of what we can offer people at this point. I guess the bottom line is that God is allowing us to provide those resources we know have been an encouragement to us and hopefully will be an encouragement to others. That's really the challenge for us. As we move down the road and opportunities like that are presented, then obviously we'd take a real close look and see what additional ways we can use to help people.

Wright

Do you have any greater visions for Outreach of Hope now?

Dravecky

I think as we look at the vision of our ministry—the real burning desire for David and Jan Dravecky—there was a point in time in our lives where we wanted to see this ministry grow, where we wanted to expand the ministry, and where we wanted to branch off into other areas. A lot of that was based on our own intentions. Not that they were bad, but as we began to spend more time seeking God—really wanting to know where He wanted us to go with this ministry—we also sought wisdom from our Board that we respect and are very grateful for. Our vision is to continue doing what we do with excellence and encouraging people one person at a time. We want to be effective in what we do today and we want to be effective tomorrow as well.

Wright

So if our readers wanted to get involved with Outreach of Hope and support you, your wife, and your organization, how would they do that?

Dravecky

We are a 501(c)(3) non-profit organization, so people can make tax-deductible contributions to the Outreach of Hope. We actually have a web site that has just been redesigned that we would love for people to visit. The address is www.outreachofhope.org. Listed there is what Outreach of Hope offers in the way of resources and ministry. We post *The Encourager* magazine on the Web site so people can get it right from there. The web site is a very unique way in which people can take a look at the ministry and then preferably consider how they might help.

There's more than just one way of helping us. Obviously, we want people to pray for what we are doing. This business of crossing over that sacred line into the journey of pain and suffering with others is very serious. We need God's direction and God's strength as we deal with each individual. We welcome prayer support.

We are a member of the Evangelical Council for Financial Accountability. We believe it's very important for us to be held accountable with the resources and the investments people give toward this ministry as we reach out and encourage families who are hurting. Obviously, we welcome whatever God would lead people to do in particular as it relates to participating in our ministry and what we are doing. We're very grateful for it.

Wright

Let me read a quote that was taken from something you have written. This is a direct quote, "You know that you need a savior. All you have to do is take God at His word and believe His promise in John 3:16." And then you go on to say, "It is that simple and that hard because you first have to do what many others have done before you." Can you tell us a little bit about what you mean?

Dravecky

Well, you know, I think response to that is really twofold. For me, as I was on my journey seeking God, the one thing I had to acknowledge was that His Word is the truth. I think it's so important for people to recognize that. First of all, there's a huge question over the authenticity of Scripture. Many people question God because they just don't know that the Bible is true. As a result, I think it's very important for people to come face to face with the reality of the truth of God's Word.

Once you come to that place, you have to accept what's in it—between the front and back covers. As you begin to go on that journey, it's very important to ask the right questions and in seeking those answers that you go to the Source of truth for those answers.

The reality is that, as simple as the Gospel message is, it is the most profound message in the universe because it is our only hope. What people have to come to realize is that God's Word is the truth, and that it provides life for people who are seeking true meaning and purpose in life. As they seek that out—as they go to the Scriptures—they will find what Jesus has done for all of us at the cross. Through His death and through His resurrection, what He has really done is set us free from the bondage of sin.

I think one of the most incredible things for me as I was on that journey was to really come face to face with my sinfulness. Once I was able to do that, the rest, as they say, is history. I knew what my choice (and the reality was I had no other choice) was Jesus and it was accepting what He had done by giving up His life so that I could have life.

I can't tell you how valuable that has been in my life, especially battling with cancer. My real hope is not in whether or not I survive, it's in knowing where I'm going when I move from this life to the next. So, I believe that it really does revolve around those two issues—coming face to face with the reality and the truth of Scripture, and then as you do that, recognizing who you are before this awesome God. We're all sinners, yet God through His Son, Jesus Christ, has wiped out that sin if we can respond to His call by accepting His Son into our lives and confessing that sin.

Wright

As I stated before, growing up in a Christian home, of course, I always prayed. But I kind of relegated prayer to helping me get through the math test and things like that, you know? I've got a teenage daughter and I hope I didn't pass that on. But the whole concept of trying to get God to change His mind in intercessory prayer was always a little scary for me even though I continued doing it. But in the last several years, I certainly can't deny what is clearly there in front of me when so many of my friends have faced such hard times in every conceivable area of their lives.

What do you think about prayer? Do these people you are reaching through your Outreach program request prayer?

Dravecky

They sure do request prayer. As a matter of fact, we offer prayer. Our prayer ministry is at the center of who we are. When families are referred to our ministry, once we gather all their information and get a little background on them, the first thing we do is to pray for them. We pray for their journey. We pray for what they are facing. We plead on behalf of them before God.

Prayer is a huge question in the Christian community as well as abroad—can we really change the mind of God? I don't know how to answer this except to hold up the example of Jesus when He said, "Not my will but Thy will be done" (Matthew 26:42). I want to be able to trust God in my prayer that His will is worked out in the lives of these people.

Sometimes we may not like what His will is, but at the same time He is a sovereign God, and I have trust and I believe that He knows what's best for me. He knows what's best for my family. Ultimately, what I've come to realize on this journey—particularly as it relates to prayer—is that I just want to share my heart with God. I want God to know what's going on inside of me. I can't hide anything from Him, and He desires to fellowship with me. Prayer is one way in which I can fellowship with Him.

For us, the beauty of what we're able to do through the Outreach of Hope is intercede on behalf of people who are desperate, who are hurting, and who need a healing touch from God. Sometimes that healing touch is the human touch that comes from the heart, not necessarily the body. The most important thing we have come to realize and acknowledge here at the Outreach is there is an incredible healing God offers to each and every one of us.

Wright

There has to be power there. One of the things that was a deciding factor (if not *the* deciding factor) for me was that He must have had charisma and intelligence. I mean, He preached to thousands of people and they followed Him around. The only thing—as far as I can ascertain—that His disciples ever asked Him to do in His entire life was, "Lord, teach us how to pray" (Luke 11:1). So, they must have seen the power He had access to.

Dravecky

Yes, there is power in prayer. As I said before, the greatest healing of all comes through the new life God offers through His Son, Jesus

Christ. The most incredible miracle in the universe is becoming a fol-
lower of Jesus, and then in doing so, you become a part of God's
family. When that happens, you become part of a family that has
worth beyond the comprehension of this universe. This makes us very
special regardless of whether or not we *feel* special in the midst of our
pain and suffering. It's a hope we can cling to—a hope we can hold on
to during the journey of pain and suffering when the doubts enter in,
the fear comes in, the worry takes place, and the frustration exists.

In my opinion, God allows us to experience all of those things. He
created us. We're not robots—we're human beings. He wired us with
all those emotions. The challenge for us is to move from that place to
a place of really resting in Him and experiencing His comfort and His
encouragement on that journey, and really trusting Him. That's the
challenge for all of us because we are human.

Wright

I do have a last question for you, and before I ask you the question, I really do want to thank you for spending this much time with
me today in *Speaking of Faith*. I've certainly learned a lot, and it's
really been exciting for me to talk with you.

Dravecky

I appreciate that.

Wright

How did you manage to hold on to your faith during the tough
times when all of those bad things were happening over which you
had little or no control?

Dravecky

You know what? My wife likes to describe it this way (and I think
I can relate to this in my own personal journey): The truth is I don't
know if I had the strength to hold on. Our grip was really tight in the
beginning because we were strong enough, but then all of a sudden,
as we continued on in the journey, we lost strength and our grip got a
little looser. The next thing you know, it had become so overwhelming—the pain was so overwhelming, and the doubts, and worry
became so overwhelming—that what ended up happening was we lost
our grip. People who experience what we went through can lose their
grip to a point where they don't hold on anymore.

The beautiful thing that takes place is that when you fall, you fall into the arms of God. Here's how that happens—I believe it takes place in three ways: God uses people and surrounds us with His love through His people. They are an extension of His hands. Even when I didn't feel like praying, I knew others were praying for me and through prayer something special happened. I don't know how to explain it. It was understanding that not only were there people there to encourage me to reveal God's faithfulness, but I could cry out to God knowing that He would hear my prayer. As a result, those people became even more important because they were the answer to my prayer to God for the strength, the encouragement, and the comfort I needed.

Last, but not least, what I held on to more than anything else were the Scriptures—God's Word—in particular in First John 5:11–13, *"He who has the Son has life. He who does not have the Son does not have life. These things I tell you so that you may know you have eternal life."* When you are face-to-face with your own mortality, the assurance of salvation and eternal life is critical to holding on to hope.

Wright

Well, what a great conversation. Dave, again, thank you so much for talking to me today.

Dravecky

It was my pleasure. Thank you.

Wright

Today we have been talking with Dave Dravecky. Dave Dravecky was a successful baseball pitcher in the big leagues. He is a successful cancer survivor and is, and as we've found out today, a true child of God. Thank you very much, Dave.

Dravecky

Thank you.

About The Author

Dave is in great demand as a speaker, addressing a wide variety of audiences across the country. His messages range from motivational to inspirational to evangelical. Through his experience, he addresses loss and suffering, faith, encouragement and hope, reaching out to others and saying goodbye to the past.

Dave Dravecky
www.davedrevecky.org